T0065597

A Deed in Your Day

Scribbler II

WESTBOW
PRESS®
A DIVISION OF THOMAS NELSON
& ZONDERVAN

Scripture quotes marked (KJV) are taken from the King James Version of the Bible.

Scripture quotations marked (AMP) taken from the Amplified® Bible (AMP), Copyright © 2015 by The Lockman Foundation Used by permission. www.Lockman.org

This book is a work of non-fiction. Unless otherwise noted, the author and the publisher make no explicit guarantees as to the accuracy of the information contained in this book and in some cases, names of people and places have been altered to protect their privacy.

WestBow Press books may be ordered through booksellers or by contacting:

WestBow Press
A Division of Thomas Nelson & Zondervan
1663 Liberty Drive
Bloomington, IN 47403
www.westbowpress.com
1 (866) 928-1240

Because of the dynamic nature of the Internet, any web addresses or links contained in this book may have changed since publication and may no longer be valid. The views expressed in this work are solely those of the author and do not necessarily reflect the views of the publisher, and the publisher hereby disclaims any responsibility for them.

Any people depicted in stock imagery provided by Thinkstock are models, and such images are being used for illustrative purposes only. Certain stock imagery © Thinkstock.

ISBN: 978-1-5127-5478-0 (sc)
ISBN: 978-1-5127-5479-7 (e)

Library of Congress Control Number: 2016913936

Print information available on the last page.

WestBow Press rev. date: 09/12/2016

For
My Family
and
Pastor & Mrs. Warren Green

Acknowledgments

Jesus, thank You for salvation and all the blessings and care You have brought into my life. You are at the heart of this book.

I would like to thank all who were part of the narratives.

Thanks to all who will take the time to read these praise reports. I pray you will see the working of God in your life and write your own book someday.

Cheryl Duvall, thank you. You encouraged me to take these vignettes beyond the planning stage.

Thanks to all pastors who prepare a table of God's good word to nourish our souls.

Pastor Kenneth O'Connell, thanks for the assurance that the gospel will go forth unchanged to future generations.

A special thanks to Pastor and Sister Green, my parents in the Lord. You were there faithfully serving the Lord when I needed to see people who exampled their message. Small things make **big** differences.

Praise and testimony services are things of the past. But sometimes, "It feels like fire shut up in my bones!" This book is my outlet!

I am writing this to share, from the depths of my being, some of the beautiful things God has done in my own days. He is the same yesterday, today, forever.

Paraphrased King James or Amplified Bible

Deut. 6: 11-12
11: ...when you have eaten and are full (plenty)
12: ...**Then beware lest you forget the Lord**, ...

Deuteronomy 6: 20-21
20: When your son asks you in the future, "What do these statutes, judgments, testimonies, that the Lord our God has commanded you mean?"
21: You shall say to your son, "We were ...**in bondage**...and the **Lord** brought us out...with a mighty hand."

Deuteronomy 6: 4-7
4: ...**The Lord our God is one Lord**.
5: ...love the Lord your God with all your heart, ...might... soul...
6: ...these words, which I command you today, shall be **in your heart**:
7: ...you shall teach them **diligently** to your children, talk of them when you're sitting in your house, walking "by the way", when you go to bed, and when you get up.

Deuteronomy 6:24-25
24: ...fear the Lord our God, for **our good** always, that He might preserve us alive...

25: …it shall be **for our righteousness**, if we do as the Lord our God has commanded us.

Deuteronomy 5:29
"O that there were such an heart in them that they would fear me and keep all my commandments always, **that it might be well with them and with their children for ever**!"

Contents

Dallas

Rio Grande Valley

Moving On

Texas Tumbleweed

In *What-so-ever State I Am*

Called to be Elsewhere

Beginning to Understand

Early Years

Uncle Charlie

Dad was from a large family. He had eleven brothers and sisters. I was told that Grandma lost a couple of babies somewhere during the birthing of this large family. Grandpa died of pneumonia when he was in his early fifties. That left Grandma to raise the children who were not yet married, which was most of them, alone. Dad was twenty at that time, but he had the largest responsibility for helping Grandma take care of his siblings.

Most of the married children eventually moved to California in search of "greener pastures". Grandma decided to take her youngest four and follow them. Dad and another brother or two remained in Arkansas. Dad married at twenty-one years old and started his own family. He thought of moving there too, but decided that he didn't consider California a "fit place" to raise a family.

When I was four years old, my family of four lived in the country in Arkansas. We had not yet started attending church. One night, Daddy woke Mom, my brother, and me in the middle of the night. He told us to get up and get dressed. A large, bright light had flashed in the window of our bedroom and startled Mom and Dad awake. I was small but remember all this happening. They couldn't figure out where the light had come from. No vehicles were nearby. We eventually went back to bed and to sleep.

A few days later, we were notified that my uncle had been killed in California. Someone had flashed a spotlight in his eyes causing him to lose control as he rode his motor scooter. He hit a utility pole and was killed. Dad was devastated. His brother was only nineteen years old. Dad thought the bright light was a warning from God that the accident had happened or was about to happen.

The loss of his brother had a lasting impact on Dad. He never allowed any of his own children to own a motorcycle or ride with anyone else on theirs if he had "a say" in the matter.

Shortly after my uncle's death, we were invited to attend church with my aunt's family. We went, and we continued to attend even after those who invited us had moved out of state.

I remember the night that God filled my daddy with the Holy Spirit. I didn't understand what was happening to my dad as he wept and praised God. I watched closely, and when he opened his eyes and put his arms down, I ran to him and reached up for him to take me up. He picked me up and held me so tightly that I wondered what had happened to him. He seemed very happy and was smiling, but tears were still streaming down his face.

That turned out to be a life-changing event for our family. Dad quit smoking and "cussing". That was for sure a positive, since I was starting to pattern my habits after his. He was my daddy. I just knew that if he did something it must be alright. I bought little white candy cigarettes with red ends and pretend smoked them. Mom said I once ran into the house to tell her the pigs had come into the yard. I did not refer to them as pigs. Dad was ready to punish me, but she reminded him that he had called them the name I used, and I was just saying what I thought they were. Someone is watching each of our lives, though we sometimes feel that nobody knows or cares.

Thank God for the life-changing Holy Spirit that makes us new creatures in Him. We need Jesus!

Grandpa and Grandma

We lived in Arkansas when I was small. Our house was a large two-story house with a large hall and staircase between the rooms on each side. For a child, the house was a fascinating place and held lots of places to explore. It was home to three families at one time. My grandparents, Mom's parents, lived in one side downstairs. My newly married aunt and uncle lived in the other side downstairs. My dad, mom, brother and I lived in the upstairs rooms. It was fun for me to live around so many relatives and close enough to visit my grandparents every day.

My grandparents kept us if Mom and Dad were working. I learned a lot from them. Grandma baked little pies and biscuits kid-sized just for me. Grandpa taught us a little bit of how to work. He sometimes built shelves, chicken houses, or other small carpentry items. He would invite my brother to hand him tools or pieces of wood. Grandpa called this "piddling". One day, Grandpa said to my brother, "Do you want to go piddle for a while?" My brother had caught on to this routine and replied, "Grandpa, that piddling runs into work!" That line was a family joke for years. But, we were learning and starting to know that we could make a worthwhile contribution to family projects.

I was too small to really do much. Sometimes I was allowed to "set the table". I loved my grandma so much. I would climb up in a kitchen chair and talk nonstop as she prepared dinner for the whole family. She sometimes cooked the bread a little longer than necessary and would say that she "got busy talking" to me and burned the bread. So, what did these all important conversations cover? Well, we had a lot of important things to discuss.

Another day Grandma worked outside in the backyard washing on a rub-board, boiling our clothes in a large, black wash kettle, and putting "bluing" in clothes to make them white. As she worked, she found a little bird nest with a few blue bird eggs and showed them to me. So, that was probably one topic of discussion; or maybe, blue color making clothes white!

Grandma was always neatly groomed and put a fresh apron on to protect her dress from getting smudged during preparation of the three full meals a day she prepared, or the outdoor laundry chores. She was also busily training up her little granddaughter. She would say, "Come and sit on the dresser stool and let me comb and brush your hair." Sometimes it was hard for me to submit to that because of the many work/play things I needed to do. Then she would say, "You don't want tangles and rats' nests in your hair like "Poochy". Poochy was a neighbor girl about my age. She was often seen running about with tangled, unbrushed hair. That was all it took. I would quickly sit on the stool to let her comb and braid my hair into, sometimes too-tight, braids. As a little follow-up note, Poochy grew up to be a very pretty girl that I wouldn't have minded looking like at all.

I became so much a Grandma's girl that I once faked being asleep when Dad came to take me home. I got to spend the night sleeping between Grandpa and Grandma. That only happened once. When Dad arrived home without me, Mom cried, and it never happened again.

My grandma wouldn't be anything special in the world's eyes. She dressed most days in a simple, but clean, cotton dress over which she wore a long, bibbed apron. She pulled her straight, thin hair back in a chignon. She was neat and clean both in her life, grooming, and housekeeping. She would sit in her "rocker", if she caught a few extra minutes during the day, and read her Bible or pray. As I grew up, I always felt better about my problems if I knew Grandma was praying for me.

I have many times said that if I patterned my life after any person, it would be Grandma. When I think of her, I think of purity, cleanliness, unselfishness, and love. The last time I read **The Book,** it still said those are some qualities that will be in heaven.

I was told of an earlier time in Grandma's life when she suffered hardships that would have "broken" a weaker person. She made clothes for her children and then for her "grands" when they came along. She raised gardens and cooked the game that Grandpa and the men of the family brought home. She set a table fit for a king out of what God provided. She did that patiently and lovingly.

But once, she planted her garden where she found a nice garden spot away from the house. She would go there regularly to chop the weeds from the tender young plants that would soon feed a hungry family and provide "canned" food for the winter months.

Grandpa used to drink before I was born. The family said he would do totally ridiculous things when he was drinking. It was bad enough that he spent his family's money on liquor, but he didn't stop there. He would scream, yell, and curse. His children were afraid of what else he might do. No wonder liquor is sometimes called "spirits"! The "spirits" people sometimes seem to show when drinking are definitely not the kind one wants. Such was the case with Grandpa when he used to drink. He also smoked. It was all an embarrassment to his family.

After Grandma planted her garden and had it up and growing well, she told Grandpa one day that she was going to work in the garden for a while. She got her bonnet (The bonnet, a story in itself: made of cotton material that had a flap that hung down over her neck in back and a starched-stiff brim that shaded her face from the sun) and told Grandpa where she was going. Grandpa said, "Ain't no need to go. You ain't got no garden." She went on but learned that she, indeed, had no garden because he had chopped it to the ground in a fit of anger and frustration. He was trying to quit smoking. He later asked her to plant it again. She forgave and went with him and replanted.

I think most people would have told him to plant it himself, since it was he who had chopped it down, but Grandma was a humble, forgiving person. Grandpa was eventually able to stop smoking. Grandma's forgiveness and prayers probably had a lot to do with that. Grandpa had a lot of faith in Grandma's prayers. One can see why.

Thank God for grandparents. If you are blessed to be one, you are blessed indeed! What an opportunity to shine for Jesus.

When Grandma passed away at 74 years of age, the scriptures read for her were *Proverbs 31:10-31*. They were definitely appropriate.

A Loose Tooth

Many times God comes down to deal with us on our own level, much as a parent does with a child. Children just learning about their world have lots of questions. Parents have answers for their children, and God has answers for His.

I was around ten or eleven years old and for some reason still had a baby molar tooth that had not come out. It was a bit loose, but it stubbornly stuck around. I was terrified of letting Mom and Dad get it out. They had given me stories of kids getting one end of a string tied to an offending tooth and the other end to a doorknob or heavy object and then yanked out by sudden movement. I could not imagine going through such a horrible thing; or maybe the problem was that I could imagine, but I wasn't about to let it happen to me if there was another way out.

Dentists were out of the question in our poverty-level family of six. One only went to a dentist when a tooth ached so much there was no other remedy than to have it removed.

I waggled and wiggled the tooth as had worked for me with past teeth, but still it went nowhere. This one was very stubborn! Eventually, it interfered with my eating. I knew I was coming down to a show-down with my parents' methods if I didn't get it out, and soon.

I prayed one night as I went to bed, "God, if there really is a God, just let this tooth fall out on my tongue." I prayed that way because I was afraid of swallowing it if it came out in my sleep. I went to bed and went soundly asleep. Sometime in the night I was startled awake! My tooth was totally out and on my tongue! I prayed a very specific prayer, and I got a very specific answer. God actually gave me several very specific and merciful answers to that prayer. We must believe that God is, "...and that He is a rewarder of them that diligently seek Him" (Hebrews 11:6). This was my first step to a personal relationship with Jesus. I had gone to church since I was five, but I needed to know Him and that He knew me. I guess that was the beginning of my knowing that God is with me and I can speak directly to Him. He will answer my prayers directly.

He has been hearing and answering my prayers ever since that time. Praise His holy name! Sometimes I get a yes, sometimes a no, and sometimes a wait or a maybe; however, I am learning to trust Him to work things for my good.

Big Creek

My parents, my two little brothers and I had been to church in town. There came a storm with drenching rain while the services were going on. It was mostly over by the time we started the twelve miles to our home in the country. I usually slept as Dad drove and did so this night until we reached the "Big Creek" bridge. The creek was a man-made, very deep creek to accommodate the water that gushed down out of the hills into the flat rice land. There was a wooden bridge on wooden pilings that crossed it on the road that led to our house.

As we neared the bridge, I was wide awake! I watched as Dad stopped the car and walked to the edge of the bridge. We could see the dark, rushing, inky water just a few inches under it. I was hoping that he would decide not to risk crossing. We could always go the long way around. He knelt down and examined the bridge. He got up and walked a little way onto it. The water under it was gushing downstream. I knew that the bridge had washed out in the past and might do so this time. There had even been a family that drowned in this very creek because of a washed out bridge. The story had been on the radio news. Dad returned to the car and announced that we would try it. I thought, "I can't even swim and neither can Mom and the boys!" Dad started the car, and we slowly made our way across. I was almost coming out of my skin with fear! On the other side, I gave a sigh of relief.

Thinking back to that incident, I am sure that Dad was praying as he knelt by the bridge to examine it. I was doing my own share of praying in the car! I can imagine Jesus guiding our little family through the peril.

The next day we drove back to look. The bridge was gone and the fields near the creek were flooded. God has lots of experience dealing with water. I have read that He made waters a wall on the right and left side with dry land in between (Exodus 14:22, Amplified Bible).

What a blessing to be able to call on the Lord at any time.

Tornado

I was at school and Mom and my little brothers were at home in our small, four-room frame house. The school was made of more sturdy materials, so I worried more for Mom and my brothers than myself as a fierce storm passed through our tiny town and moved into the country. I rode the school bus home, almost afraid to look as we neared our house. Thank God! The house still stood.

Mom described what happened at home. She had been taking a nap when my little brother (about four years old at the time) came to her and said, "Momma, there's an old black cloud coming." Mom jumped to her feet just as the winds hit! She said the front door blew open. She grabbed one little son in each arm and threw herself against it to try to close it.

The storm was moving fast and soon was over. They went to see if the outside buildings were still standing. The chicken house had been blown away and the few chickens were walking around on the ground looking even more confused than usual. My little brother discovered that the "outhouse" had been blown away. He exclaimed to Mom, "It blew our toilet away. Daddy's really gonna be mad!"

Dad managed to get home and learn about it without really being mad, and we all rejoiced and were thankful that we were still a complete family.

Dr. Jesus

Swollen glands in my neck started this episode. I was very ill and ran an extremely high fever. Mom slept with me at night for fear of what might happen to me. I could not bear to lie flat on my back and would have Mom prop me up to sleep.

Poor families like ours didn't have insurance in those days and tried to care for their sick children at home. Dad took me to our elderly country doctor. He didn't know what was wrong with me but treated me with penicillin shots every day for a week. I was not getting better.

One night I was running a very high fever and Mom was sleeping with me to keep an eye on me. She said my skin burned to the touch. I remember trying to wake and couldn't. I knew I wanted to wake up, but I only felt alternating smooth, folding sensations and rough jagged ones in my head. Finally, I was able to wake.

The last day of the illness, I told Mom to call my dad to come and pray for me. He was already outside getting ready to go to work. He came back to where I was propped up on the sofa for the day and prayed for me. He then went on to work. By the time he returned that evening, I was up and feeling much better.

I believe we all learned a lesson, or some lessons, from God in that time. My parents had grown cold spiritually. We were not going to church as we had in the past. I think God showed my dad that he needed to be ready and able to call on God at a moment's notice for his children. He also saw that during the years he had kept his child in church, *that* child had learned who to call on when desperately in need. It was not a doctor, although the doctor tried. It was the Creator, Jesus, who paid for my healing with the cruel stripes that He suffered. I think we all saw that we needed to be in church where we could learn about our Lord and worship Him.

His mercy is everlasting.

Little Brother's Close Call

After my illness, we had another illness in our family. My little brother was only about four years old. It was cold winter time, and we had a roaring fire in the wood stove in the living room. Mom and Dad frequently depended on me to help care for my little brothers. This night Mom noticed that my brother had wet his pants and told me to change him. I started to, but he refused to allow it. Mom and Dad intervened with threats of a spanking and then discovered that he was hiding a terrible secret. He was swollen totally out of proportion and turning dark on his genitals. Dad grabbed him up and headed to the emergency room. That was twelve miles away. By the time they got there, he was getting gangrene. He was quickly sent to surgery for an emergency circumcision. His jaws began locking during the procedure, and the nurse got some pretty badly chewed up fingers trying to prevent him from swallowing his tongue. I suspect that Dad did some powerful praying that night.

We waited at home to hear what had happened to our little brother. We had no phone, so Dad couldn't call to update us on what was going on.

He survived by God's mercy! He came home to us with instructions for his care. It was a most pitiful sight. He would half-sit and half-lie in the armchair with a cover draped over him. He could not bear to have clothing touch him. I remember grieving for him and rushing off the school bus every afternoon to see if he was better.

I guess Dad had finally had enough. He went to Illinois to find a job, leaving us to cry when Mom read us his homesick letters about how much he missed us. We were missing him just as much or more. He would send for or come to get us when he had a place for us. God provided, and we were able to join him.

We had a nice place to live and a good church to attend. That was the church where I was baptized in the lovely name of Jesus for the remission of my sins. I was about twelve by then.

Yes, there is a God! In His mercy and love He is working for you and your poor, pitiful little family that most people hardly notice. He notices and loves those who need Him and call on Him in time of trouble. Sometimes He answers before we call because He sees our need.

> *"Bless the Lord, O my soul, and all that is within me, bless His holy name!"* (Psalm 103:1)

Snakes Alive!

My family lived in rice country for several years when I was a child. My brother and I played with a friend in a small ditch in front of our little frame house. I don't ever remember seeing a snake in the yard or ditch. We might have been near some and didn't know it, but one day we ran inside to tell Daddy that there was a turtle in the attic above the front door. I was three and my brother five, so that is what we thought it was. Water moccasins were plentiful because of the flooded rice fields and that is what it actually was. God had kept us safe!

We later lived in the two-story house where three families of us once lived. This house was on sandy, dry land. The snakes there were mostly rattlesnakes. Mom sent me to get a washcloth from a dresser drawer. When I opened the drawer, coiled on top of the washcloths was a rattlesnake. Dad killed it.

At the same house, I played house with a little friend in the storm cellar. Dad closed the door to the cellar during a rain. A few days later he opened it to let the cellar air out. Out from under the door crawled a rattlesnake. …end of the playhouse in the cellar!

We moved back to rice country into a different frame house than before. Mom discovered a water moccasin hanging out of an article of clothing in one of our closets. Later, I panicked when I discovered a moccasin crawling down a facing by the back door in the kitchen. Who knows how many were in the house but never discovered!

Dad sent my older brother and me to pick black berries one day. He was about twelve, and I was around ten years old. The berry vines were on a large ditch bank. We picked for a while, but I wasn't getting much done for fear of seeing a snake. We finally went home. Mom and my little brothers went to the same area to fish a few days later. They took along our snake-killing dogs. A large snake came up the ditch bank and was headed toward Mom and the babies. Mom didn't see it. The dog, Blackie, saw it and grabbed it and started shaking it to kill it, but it bit him in the process. By the time they walked home, Blackie was dying. We children stood on the porch begging Daddy to do something and watched as our little dog died.

God was our refuge in all these cases.

> *The angel of the Lord encampeth round about them that fear him and delivereth them. (Psalms 34:7)*

City Dangers

I wrote earlier that things were better for us when we moved to Illinois. We had better housing, food, clothing, and a good church. But, the city had its own dangers.

I baby sat my little three and five-year-old brothers and prepared meals for Mom and Dad while they worked at a motel about a block from our house.

In the course of Dad's work at the motel, he met a strange couple. They had a dark past and probably present. Dad had a dream or vision about a crime the woman had committed. He let her know about it. I guess he hoped to try to get them to come to church. She admitted that it was true, but they did not come to church.

One day as I cooked lunch and the little boys played outside in the yard, the couple came to our back door and asked if Daddy was home. Dad had discussed them at home, so I knew to be afraid of them. I heard movement in the living/dining area of the house, but was afraid to leave them at our back door. Only a hooked screened door separated me from them, and I was afraid they would at any moment jerk the door open and come in after us. Almost instantly, Dad showed up behind them. He had been keeping an eye on them as they headed toward our house. He talked with them for a few minutes and they left.

Mom came home for lunch which had been on the table for a few minutes when the couple arrived. Mom helped herself to some turnip greens and said, "Wup!" She felt small pieces of glass in her mouth full of food. Shards were visible in the bowl of greens on the table. We dumped the food and ate something else.

The couple checked out of the motel, and we didn't see them again while we lived there.

I think Dad would have been wise to have kept his warning dream/vision to himself. He could have invited them to church and let God make the revelation there. It might or might not have brought about repentance, but the family probably would not have been as directly involved.

God knows if or when people are ready to live right. Those apparently were not ready. Only God's mercy kept us safe.

* * * * * * * *

Another city danger took place as I walked the twelve blocks home from school. I walked with a little friend. We dressed in warm clothing and wore scarves over our hair to keep our ears warm. We were walking in snow most of the time. Outside temps were well below freezing.

A particular gang of six or eight kids from our school discovered that we walked the same street home every day and started to follow close behind us and harass us as we walked. They would say things and jerk our scarves off our heads. The ring leader of this group was a beautiful little eighth grade girl. Her mom had died a short time earlier and her dad was left to raise her alone. He probably had no idea of her involvement in this. There were boys and girls in the group. They fed off each other's wickedness.

After a couple of episodes of their meanness, I reported to my dad. He paid a visit to my school without telling me he was about to do that. He spoke with the superintendent and explained that he would be watching our route home. If this occurred again he would take matters into his own hands. That was the last time it happened, to us.

A girl who had to walk through the park to get home was attacked a few days later as she went home. The same gang knocked her to the ground and stabbed a fingernail file into her hands.

Being a "tattle tale" paid off. Dad kept watch for us for a while to make sure no one tried to retaliate. Thank God for a dad who cared enough to take time out of his busy day to take care of his child. I was blessed to have that kind of dad.

I guess Dad thought we faced snakes of one sort or another anywhere we went. He was adding this city to his list of places "not fit to raise kids". By the time I was fourteen, we were back in Arkansas.

Daylight in the Night

I had been to a youth camp with a group of kids from my church. We returned to my hometown and I went to a friend's house to wait for the guy I dated to take me home. He arrived around 7 p.m. We went for a snack and then drove around for a while. I had to be home by 10:30 and lived in the country, so we headed toward my house around 10:00. His curfew was 11:00 p.m. On the way to my house, it was suddenly light enough to see down the road in both directions and out across the fields. There was no visible source of light. It was just light all around—very strange.

As I look back on that incident, I sometimes wonder if God was warning me not to get involved with this young man whom I later married. At the time he was handsome, well groomed, intelligent, from a good family and a religion very much like mine. I now know that marriage to one with exactly the same religious views is extremely important. Thirteen years of marriage and a divorce later, he was anything but what I had dreamed of marrying.

God's protecting hand stayed upon me even when I was astray. His mercy endures forever! Thank God!

By the time the marriage was over, I was ill both physically and emotionally. Many times I wondered if I would ever really be okay again. I look back and see that God was carrying me when I was so distraught that I didn't really even know how to pray for myself.

Thank you, God, for putting me back on the Potter's wheel and making me a "new vessel" as pleased You. You could have just thrown me aside as a broken piece of clay, not worth saving; but you rescued me and started me over again. I adore You! "To whom much is forgiven, loves much."

Jeremiah 18:4 Luke7:47 Isaiah 54

Learning That I Must Have Jesus

Tornado Again

This tornado was much more deadly. It came in the night. My dad was out of town working. My mom and my young teenaged brothers were home alone. As the storm hit, Mom and the boys went into a middle bedroom and got down between my brothers' twin beds and clung to each other and prayed. The windows in the house were broken out and the many big trees in the yard uprooted. The house was moved about an inch and a half over on its foundation. A long 2" x 4" was driven into the side of the house and stuck out at an angle. Mom and the boys were safe.

Across the street from Mom's house the two-story house lost its top floor but all escaped alive. My little brother went with the teenage boy from that house to look for people who might not have been as blessed. They picked their way through downed trees and power lines on the hill where they lived to the flat land a few miles down the road. The houses that had once been there were gone. The family of four from one of them was found dead in the field nearby.

"The angel of the Lord encampeth round about them that fear him, and delivereth them."
(Psalms 34: 7)

God Reveals Secrets

The king answered…Of a truth it is, your God is a
God of gods, and a Lord of kings, and a revealer of
secrets, (Daniel 2:47)

…Before that Philip called thee, when thou wast
under the fig tree, I saw thee (John 1:48).

My husband worked at night on the police department. He was preparing for work one night and I was observing. I commented to him that I had a really weird feeling, and that it was sort of like I sometimes felt before a big storm. Only, this day was clear with no storms in the forecast. He just laughed it off and went on to work.

I prayed for his safety always, so I did this night also.

The next morning when he came in, he told me that he came very close to dying that night. He and his coworker had arrested a man, frisked him, and were in the process of cuffing and placing him in the patrol car when he came out of nowhere with a switchblade knife and was well on his way to slicing up a cop! My husband grabbed the wrist that was holding the knife and squeezed with all his strength until the knife fell to the pavement. A couple of experienced officers returned to the station badly shaken and a lot more cautious from then on. They could not imagine where he had been hiding that knife. God saw it before the shift started! Once again, by God's mercy, he lived to see another day...a space of time to repent...

God is merciful and longsuffering, not willing that **any** perish but come to repentance.

Little Ellen & Separation of Church and State

I taught school near a military base for two years. My first year there had me teaching third grade (self-contained) to mostly children of military personnel. It was truly a multicultural teaching experience.

I taught a beautiful little girl in that group named Ellen. She had shoulder-length, straight, dark brown hair and large, expressive, almost black eyes with long dark lashes. Beautiful!

One day it came up a terrible storm. Our classroom had windows on two sides, so even if the kids got on the floor in their storm positions, we had little or no protection. I was feeling my responsibility heavily that day. I knew I could not lead my babies in prayer, though I felt the need. We had all kinds of religious beliefs in that classroom. If a child of mine had been there with a different teacher, I would not have wanted the teacher leading my child to pray in a manner perhaps very different, or to a different god than the God it had been taught to believe. I would have wanted them to allow my child to pray the way he/she had been taught to pray at home or in my own church. I was trying to practice the "do unto others" rule.

Ellen looked at me with her beautiful eyes that were showing a lot of fear and said, "I'm scared." The rest of the class also looked scared of the rapidly approaching black cloud but said nothing. I said, "Do you go to church, Ellen?" She replied that she did. I asked her what her church taught her to do when she was afraid.

I went on with what I had to do and silently whispered a prayer for our safety.

A moment later, when I looked over at Ellen, she had her eyes closed and her little hands folded in silent prayer. Soon she opened her eyes and seemed perfectly calm as the storm passed through.

That is what I call child-like faith. God, help us all to have it.

Whenever, Wherever —
God Answers Prayer

I taught third grade in the early seventies. I was a miserable teacher because my marriage was falling apart. I went to work every day just hoping to make it to the next; but I knew some way, and with God's help, I could plod on. Teaching helped me get my mind off my misery for a few hours each day. I was forced to think about children's needs and try my best to contribute to their well-being. This particular year I had quite a rowdy group and couldn't think much of me, especially while at work.

One day one of my students came down with a terrible earache. He was crying and unable to be still in class. We saw the nurse. Her office was already full of sick kids, so she called home. We were told that he would have to stay at school because his mother couldn't come to get him. I was very upset over that. I thought she should make a way, borrow a ride, do something! Her child needed her! When I realized she was definitely not coming, I thought, "What can I do? I can't teach with this going on!" Also, my heart was aching for this child. I had, had an earache before, so I knew how he must have felt. The thought came to me, "Pray for him."

I managed to get the rest of the curious class seated and started on a class project. I then took the little earache boy to the back of the room and placed a pile of our coats on the floor. I had him lie down on the coats with one coat for a pillow and my coat to cover him. He was tossing from side to side in pain. I told him to be as still as he could. I knelt on the floor beside him and placed my hand on his ear. I said a short, silent prayer that God would heal him and give him relief from the pain. I went back to teaching, all the while watching my patient. Within minutes, all the writhing and crying stopped, and he slept until we woke him to go home.

♫ Jesus loves the little children, all the children of the world. Red, yellow, black, and white, they are **precious** in His sight. Jesus loves the children of the world. ♫

The Breeze

Referring to the angels He says, (God) Who makes His angels winds, and His ministering servants flames of fire (Hebrews 1:7, Amplified Bible).

Who makes winds His messengers, flames of fire His ministers (Psalms 104:4, Amplified Bible).

One particular summer was a trying time for me. I was trying to believe my marriage could work, but it grew worse every day. I got sick that summer and required a minor surgery. My husband got a prescription for my pain from the emergency room to get me through one night. He took me to the hospital the next morning. They told me I would need to spend at least a night in the hospital after the surgery. I got through my first ever surgery fine and was put in a room with another lady.

My husband left as soon as the surgery was over and never returned until it was time to check me out. I felt so alone. The assistant pastor of my church came to pray for me. Later my 17-year-old sister-in-law came and sat with me for a couple of hours. While we talked, I noticed a really nice breeze across my bed. I was in the bed next to the windows, so I thought someone had pushed one of them open for a while. I remember thinking, "I need to have her close that window before she goes home so it won't get too chilly in here before morning." We continued to visit, and finally she went home. I realized too late that I had forgotten to ask her to close the window. I guessed I could call a nurse if it became too cold. All night I felt the breeze when I would awaken. It never changed temperatures.

The next morning the nurse came into the room ready to begin her routines, and the lady in the other bed asked her to please turn on the air conditioning. She said it had been "stuffy" in the room all night. The nurse agreed that it was stuffy in the room and turned on the air.

...Who makes His angels winds...

Years later, I would read this scripture in the Bible and understand that I had experienced it.

Another Tornado

I was always a bit afraid of bad storms. My parents raised me to go to storm shelters when one was available. You see, we grew up in part of what is known as "Tornado Alley". After hearing of the damage they could do and the lives they sometimes claimed, we were taught that God gave one "sense enough" to get out of their way when there was the option. Dad was an excellent, amateur weather man. He could look at a cloud coming and say, "Well, there's hail in that cloud. There's wind in this storm." He was pretty much always right. That was before the days of internet weather maps. He would sometimes get together with other families in our neighborhood and we would go in a shared shelter. He loved his family dearly and had no intention of getting them hurt because of a careless attitude. It seems that having a family tends to make people like that.

I lived in a house next door to my in-laws. One night I had gone to their house just because I knew it would likely be stormy. I didn't want to be home alone. I went there long before the storm began. As the lightening started in the distance, I would occasionally look out the window in the front door to see how the clouds were looking. I guess some of Dad's abilities had rubbed off on me. On one such peek out, I turned to my in-laws and said, "Well, I think this is it." I, like Dad, was pretty good at judging weather conditions. My somewhat amused father-in-law walked to the same window to have a look. He peeked out, turned to his wife and said, "You know… I think she's right."

They lived in a big two-story house in what was, at that time, a very nice neighborhood in an older part of town. It had a long, large living room with windows on two whole sides. They, for whatever reason, only got on the floor in that same room and leaned their bodies across their teenage daughter to wait out the storm. I was on my own. I joined them on the floor in front of the living-room sofa. As the storm hit, we heard the horrible roar everyone talks about with tornadoes. It grew very light at the long windows, almost like daylight outside. I started to pray for us and for my husband who was working the night shift that week. He was out somewhere in all this. We stayed down for what seemed like an eternity but was probably only minutes. I thought, "It sounds as though this hundred-plus-year-old-house could fly apart at any moment, and we would be cut to pieces with the glass from all these windows surrounding us." Finally, the roar peaked and started to subside. We got up and tried to find some light and waited for morning to investigate the damage. We were able to see by the flashes of lightening that the hundred-year-old tree in the back yard had been uprooted. It was an oak whose trunk was about as big around as a large wash tub. Daylight would reveal that its top had fallen on the side of the house, but other than that, there was no damage to either of our houses. Of course, the most important thing was that we were safe.

We knew our city of about 35 thousand people had been hit really hard and could only wait for word of how hard. An hour or so after the storm passed, my husband drove into the driveway and used his flashlight to pick his way into the house past the fallen trees and power lines. He came only to change into other clothes and go out again to help rescue people trapped, injured, or dead from the storm.

He said he was not in the tornado at all. He had been out of town at the time of the storm. He just worried that the wind might cause them to lose control of the police car they were using to transport two prisoners to jail. He was concerned that, should that take place, the crooks might get control of the weapons. Who knew what from there! We were thankful that it did not happen. They had trouble navigating through the streets blocked by fallen debris, but finally they reached their destination and processed the prisoners. After changing clothes, they were going back out to work the rest of the night protecting everyone else.

I was glad God had answered my prayers and kept us all safe. Some were not as blessed. One officer had ducked to the floorboard of his patrol car just before a board from the destroyed high school crashed through the windshield and stuck into the seat where he had just been sitting. With morning light, we learned that our whole city had pretty much been destroyed. Large beautiful homes were torn from their foundations in some areas leaving only parts of the plumbing and the foundations. There were deaths and some miracles. In one place, a family was looking for their baby. During the search, they discovered a car turned up on its end and leaning up against a utility pole. The baby sat underneath the car unharmed!

The house we were in was on a large corner lot. On the opposite corner, it looked as though all the trees in the yard had been uprooted. The house had sustained damages as well.

God is truly a very present help in trouble. We were living witnesses to that fact.

It pays to stay close to the Master. One never knows when He will be needed in a hurry. Sometimes all we have time to say is, "JESUS!" He hears that prayer too with all its implications, and He answers.

He has promised He will never leave or forsake us. I can't imagine ever wanting to forsake Him. I think winging it without Him can only be classified as recklessness and self-confident arrogance. I guess all the gamblers are not in Vegas.

Dream with Detailed Information

I have read in many places in the Holy Bible where people were given dreams/visions from God. I am fully aware that some dreams are just silly, or in some cases caused by medications, etc. However, a few times I have been spoken to in dreams/visions and have no doubt that they were from God for my information, good, or comfort and assurance.

This dream came when I was miserable and felt trapped in a situation with no way out. I had been married about twelve years and had no plans to ever be divorced. I grew up believing that marriage was for life, and no matter the rough times, you worked through them and stayed together. We would be together and end life still loving each other. However, four or five years before my divorce, I started to realize that the person I married was changing. Time after time things happened that pointed to unfaithfulness on his part. I eventually decided to confront him about it. We had agreed when we married that we would just level with each other if we ever found ourselves in such a position, regardless of whose fault it was. I was expecting such a moment at any time with the signs I was seeing. It never came.

Finally, I asked if he had decided to see someone else. He laughed it off and said of course he wasn't seeing anyone else.

He even used his knowledge of my religious beliefs to make me feel I was being unfair and nagging to even ask. Time rocked on and his time away became more frequent and the visible signs much more apparent. I would sit at home, cry, read my Bible and pray the best I knew how for an answer.

One night I dreamed that he confessed to me that he was going out with someone and told me her name. I was instantly wide awake the next morning! I sat up in bed and greeted my husband as he came in from his night shift at work. He placed his briefcase on the floor and started to unload his pockets and prepare for bed. He was surprised to see me sitting up and wide awake already. I was not, and am not, a morning person. He commented on my early awakening. I said, "I just had the strangest dream. I dreamed that you told me you were going out with someone." He did not react. I continued, trying to clearly recall, "Her name was Marian, or Marilyn, or ... Suddenly he stopped and stared at me and said, "I might as well tell you because you know. Her name is Mary Ann."

After all was out in the open, things got even worse. Eventually, I lived alone for a year waiting and hoping he would come to his senses and change. He never did. I finally called him and asked for a divorce. By then I was ill, both physically and emotionally. My heart was broken because I still loved him. God finally helped me to see that I was trying to hold on to someone I lost a long time before.

We talked. I asked why he didn't tell me when it started as we had agreed to do. He said it all started as wrong place, wrong time and wrong people; and before it was over, he found himself too deeply involved. By then, he had other problems. Then he just thought I would never find out. He said he never intended to end the marriage.

Our divorce was over quickly. We went our separate ways. Thank God we had no children to drag through such an experience.

I later realized that God was bringing me out of a life of bondage and giving me a new life. I was back on the Potter's wheel. He was making me a new vessel, **as pleased Him**.

I would like to be able to say that I have never made a mistake since then. I cannot. However, I can say that now I am very cautious and prayerful about the decisions I make. I know I must have God to direct my steps and am not capable of directing my own. The mistakes are fewer. Since then, I run to the Potter when I realize that I need a rough edge smoothed away or the special touch of the Master's hand. I throw myself on His wheel and submit to His kind and gentle hands as they mould me again and smooth away the rough edges.

Jesus truly is the best thing that has ever happened to me! I find great joy in serving Him.

Two Too Private to Share

Incident I

I went to pick up a friend to go riding around and parked in front of her house. She didn't come out at once, so I waited. Suddenly I got an overwhelming urge to leave, and fast. I started my car and left. I had no other knowledge of why until a later time when she explained. She said there were very serious family problems. She had tried to signal me from a window, but I had not seen her. Had I stayed, it would probably have ended in disaster. All signs were pointing in that direction. I am not sharing all the details because I want to protect the innocent people I care deeply for, but I can say that God took care of us.

Incident II

Breakfast being served to one sounds like a wonderful thing, right? It is not always a blessing. I had this happen to me a few times and found out there was more behind it than just good will. God gave me wisdom for handling that situation as well. Again, details will not be shared in order to protect the innocent involved and save them from embarrassment. God had His hand of protection over my life, even though I didn't even know I needed to be afraid until it was over.

Heart Irregularities/ Bleeding Ulcer

When my divorce was final, I lived one more year in the city where my in-laws lived, and then I decided there would be no peace or starting over as long as I lived in the same city where my "X" lived with all his girlfriends, children, etc. In late May, when I had fulfilled my work contract, I packed my car and a small U-Haul trailer and headed for I knew not where, but west.

My former sister-in-law was also my responsibility at the time, and she needed to get enrolled at a university in Texas to work on her Masters Degree. We headed there first.

I was ill and knew that I was. I was also stressed "to the max" with all that had been going on in my life. We spent a night at a motel on our way to her school. I told her that I had to rest and went to bed right away. My heart felt like it was flipping and flopping in a strange way. I felt somewhat better the next morning, and we went on.

In Texas, we rented an efficiency apartment. The daybeds served as our sofas during the day and as beds at night. We got her set up for school, and then she decided to go visit some friends in Mexico. She invited me to go with her, but I didn't want to leave the house, much less the country. I was sick.

I made an effort to hide my illness from her. When she went to Mexico, I had the perfect opportunity to check out what was happening to me. I hurt constantly, night and day. I hurt worse without food in my stomach, but I still hurt even when I ate. I was passing black, coffee-ground-looking material in my stool. I called a doctor for an appointment. I was told to be prepared to pay a large amount of money just to get the tests started. The lady who set the appointment said that my symptoms indicated a serious condition and that we needed to start treatment as soon as possible.

I had no job, was not certified to teach in Texas at the time, and was very ill. What a way to start a new life in my late twenties. By the time my sister-in-law returned a week later, I had made a decision to leave that city. I told her she was welcome to come along with me to wherever (???). I didn't know where I was going, but I was leaving there. The city seemed to me a college, party town where I definitely didn't fit in. I didn't fit in the church there either. It was big and I could get lost in the crowd. That was exactly what I thought I wanted to do, but God had other plans for me. He knew it was not what I needed.

I sold all my belongings except what would fit into my little, still not paid for, Chevy Nova. (In Mexico, they don't name cars Nova because it means that it won't go or won't run. ☺) I headed toward Dallas still nowhere near sure that I was going there.

Once on the highway headed north, I fell apart. I wept and wept and wept and poured out to God all that had been building for years. He was the only One who cared. I told Him that I had canceled my doctor appointment and if I died

I would just die. I asked for forgiveness for all the mistakes I had made in my life and gave what was left of it to Him.

I reached Arlington, Texas that afternoon. I checked into a motel and took stock of what I had to start with—enough money to live through the summer only and no insurance or money for medical bills.

The next morning, I got a newspaper and found and marked a few apartments in a part of town that seemed like an alright place to live. I could see that I really couldn't afford any of them. I decided it wouldn't hurt to look, so I called ahead and was shown some of them. The one I liked best was an upstairs efficiency. The owner and his family lived downstairs. His mother lived in an apartment downstairs, a young man lived in an upstairs efficiency, and I needed to rent the other. I told the owner the gospel truth. I had no job, no deposit money, and didn't know when or if I would get a job. He must have liked something about that. He allowed me to move in with no deposit. He said I could pay the deposit when or if I got a job. So it was that I had housing. God was already providing the impossible.

All summer I searched for a job. I could see that there would be no teaching job because there were plenty of already Texas certified teachers available to fill the openings. I would have to work on certification. I also searched for other kinds of work. Most employers were nice but let me know they thought I would leave them if a teaching position opened, so they wouldn't hire me. About two weeks before I knew I would have to go back to where I came from, I got a job interview with a small grocery chain. My position would be an office/clerical and checker trainer position. I would be handling large sums of cash, so I had to go for a polygraph.

I took the polygraph and answered all the questions as truthfully as I knew how. When it was over, the man who gave the test said if the people who sent me for the test didn't hire me to let him know and he would. He said he hadn't seen that kind of honesty in a long time. Before I left his office he said he wanted to suggest that I see a doctor right away. He showed me the print-out from the polygraph machine. It had recorded my heartbeat patterns. It looked strange. The following is the approximate pattern that I saw:

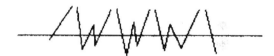

complete breaks at the tops of the tallest peaks
Heartbeat patterns and description

I have looked in books, asked nurses, and researched heartbeat patterns and have never seen anything like them anywhere. I listened to his advice but had no money for a doctor so didn't go to one.

The manager who hired me told me the polygraph guy had told him I might have serious health issues but he was going to "give me a chance". I was hired and worked for that company for three years. Over a year after I went to work, I got an appointment with a doctor. The pain in my stomach had finally gone away. The doctor didn't notice any heart irregularities. I described the pain and other symptoms I had when I moved to the area. He said it sounded like I had a bleeding ulcer but there were no indications of it then.

The Great Physician had worked again!!!

Dallas

Angel?

I got my first full-time job in Texas at a small grocery chain in Dallas. I worked varied hours and occasionally had to work on Sunday. That was not something I planned to do but was a necessity to keep the job. It became a more or less regular occurrence for a while. I was new and didn't think it wise to protest the Sunday work too much, so stayed quiet.

I had church services on Wednesday night, Sunday morning and Sunday night. Prayer meeting was on Saturday night. I soon thought that working some Sundays wasn't so bad because I could always go to the other services.

I settled into the routine.

I worked one Sunday that changed my whole outlook on the Sunday shift. I worked in the office. We cashed checks, accepted utility bills, issued the checkers their cash drawers, etc. I noticed a line of about five or six people in front of my window. I would have them out in no time at all even if they were buying money orders. I had this routine down.

One unfamiliar man near the end of the line stared intently at me as I worked. I felt the stare. I wondered why he was in line. He continued to wait in the line. When his turn came, all he wanted was some small change. As I gave him the change, he smiled and said, "I thought you would be in church." I gave him a flippant answer, "Oh, I'll be there tonight." He turned and left the store.

It struck me as strange that he would wait out a line of people just to get change for a newspaper or whatever. He could have gotten that from any one of the checkers at the front, right beside the office. They weren't even busy at that time.

I decided to have a quick look out the window to see him on the parking lot.

He sure seemed to know a lot about me. How did he know me, especially that I should be in church? I looked and tried to see him by the newspaper stands or on the parking lot, but he was nowhere in sight.

The more I thought about it, the more I was convinced that I had met my first visible angel. Close behind that thought was the idea that Jesus was certainly aware of my careless attitude about working on weekends. He was also very merciful to care enough to send me an angel rather than allow this harmful attitude to persist.

I tried harder from that point to get my weekends scheduled off. I even found the management more sympathetic to my cause than I expected them to be.

> *"But He knows the way that I take: when He has tried me, I shall come forth as gold." (Job 23:10)*

Choosing Between Jobs

I decided, after three years work at the store and getting my Texas teaching credentials, that I needed to return to the classroom. I knew I would have to get my retirement built up. There was no retirement plan in the store for me. I started my job search and prayer for the right job. When I had first arrived in Dallas, I had applied for numerous teaching positions. I was interviewed a few times but shown stacks of applications of those already certified to teach in the state and told that there was an abundance of qualified people for the positions I sought. This time, I sent applications to other parts of the state as well as the Dallas area. Maybe there would not be so many applicants outside of the city.

I heard from one job application during the summer. The superintendent called me himself and told me that it would be good if I could make the several-hundred-mile trip to visit the school. That was impossible for me because of my work hours. He called back and said that he could see that I met the qualifications and was now certified for Texas. After interviewing me by phone, he offered me the job. I accepted. When I hung up the phone I was giddy with happiness! I told my church pastor the good news. He was not as happy. He said he had been praying about this job and believed God had a job for me right in our area. I am sure my disappointment was written all over my face. He said, "As a matter of fact, you will have to choose between jobs here. Call the superintendent and withdraw your application."

I went to prayer about it and told the Lord of my disappointment and embarrassment to call and resign before I even signed the contract. I had wasted this man's time and my own. I told the Lord that I was giving this matter to Him and having nothing more to do with it. I reminded Him that this pastor was His leader for our church and this would be between Him and the pastor. I would call and withdraw the application the next day.

My hands and my heart felt heavy as I dialed the phone to relay my message to the superintendent. As I finished my apology and prepared speech, he said, "What happened? Did they offer you a big promotion at some big corporation?" I told him no and apologized again and hung up.

It was two weeks before school started and no prospects in sight. I prayed and went to ladies' prayer meetings and had them pray. At least, I still had not resigned my job at the store.

School started, and still no job was in sight. I was disappointed but not bitter. I truly had given it to God to handle and was learning to trust Him to do just that. I just waited to see how it would turn out. In my way of looking at it, I had done my part. The rest was up to God and the pastor.

Two weeks after school started, a local school called me about taking a second grade teaching position. They had a teacher who was transferring to the junior high to teach math. Would I be interested in taking over her vacancy at the elementary school? Would I ever! I started teaching my ideal grade level two weeks into the school year. I continued to work several days more at my store job so that they could hire and train my replacement. God had provided the job, but I wasn't choosing between jobs and I wondered about that.

A few months later, I got a call from another local district offering me a teaching position there. I told them I appreciated the offer but had accepted a position with another district, was pleased with it, and would remain there.

I worked for that district for six years.

Eventually I did work for four years as a third grade teacher for the second district that called.

> ...as the heavens are higher than the earth, so are
> my ways higher than your ways and my thoughts
> than your thoughts. (Isaiah 55:9)

Near Misses

I worked at the grocery store and lived on Winding Brook Circle in Dallas. Many times I would cut through a street in the golf course to Hampton Road and follow Hampton to the church I attended near I-20. On a Sunday afternoon I headed on my usual route to church. I reached the traffic signal at Hampton Road and sat waiting for the green light. The light changed and I started into the intersection to turn left onto Hampton. "Flying" over the hill on Hampton came a car loaded with people. I guess they didn't know the light was there until they topped the hill. It was impossible for them to stop for the light with the speed at which they were traveling. I saw that I was likely to be hit in the driver's side of my car by that car. I had no time to brake or to speed up. All I had time for was a "Jesus!" and that only as a thought. The car miraculously missed me and went through the light, up over the curb, into the park, and hit a tree. As I finished my turn, I saw in my rearview mirror, doors flying open on the wrecked car and people piling out on all sides. Seeing that they had survived, I went on to church badly shaken but thanking God for saving my life.

Another time, I drove some friends who were from Mexico and visiting their parents in Dallas, to the Anatole Hotel to purchase tickets to an event they wanted to attend. The man riding in my car had two or three of his children and nieces and nephews with him. After the tickets were secured and we were on our way back to their parents' business place, I was driving on a six lane street (three lanes of traffic each way). I noticed a man trying to move his car on a parking lot next to the street we were on. His lot was mostly empty of cars. He had plenty of room to move the vehicle wherever, so I was totally unprepared for what happened next. He hit the gas pedal with his car in reverse and shot up over the curb and into the street straight for us! I screamed, "Jesus!" bracing for the bang! His missing us can only be explained in that cry, "Jesus!" Sometimes that is all the praying we have time to do, but He hears and answers.

As Close as the Mention
of His Name

I always liked living in Texas, and I only moved to Arkansas because housing expenses had become so great that I could no longer afford to live there on a retiree's salary. At least, that is how I saw it. God probably saw it a different way.

Even though I was born in Arkansas, I can't say I ever really felt at home there. Some of my most unhappy memories as a child and as an adult were there. I had always told both family and friends that I would never return to live in Arkansas. I dreaded visits back so much that I would be unhappy each time a trip there approached. I wanted to see relatives, but would almost feel like getting out of my car and kissing the earth each time I crossed the AR/TX line on my return trip. That kept up for six or seven years, then before one trip home, my pastor's wife sang a song in church. I enjoyed the song, but I didn't apply its meaning to my situation at all at the time. I went to Arkansas, and again counted the days until I was supposed to leave to come home. One night, during my time there, I lay in bed thinking about how many more days I had to go before returning. My pastor's wife's song came to me. In my imagination I could hear her sweet, gentle voice singing it over and over, and finally I was singing it over and over in my head with her.

♫ He's as close as the mention of His name, Jesus, Jesus… ♫

From that night on I could go home and enjoy being with my family and going places with them without stress and worry. God is a healer of bodies, souls, minds, and emotions.

It came as a surprise, even to me, when I was happy to move to Arkansas when I retired after living in Texas for 28 years! My years back in Arkansas gave me some lasting friendships. They also gave me a chance to visit with extended family for almost eight years. I had the pleasure of watching a church grow from tiny to large there. I will always be thankful for that. I am thankful for the blessings of God in Arkansas.

Mexico

Having completed a few courses of Spanish, I wanted to get some real practice speaking with native speakers. I learned of an opportunity to participate in a class trip to study in Saltillo, Coahuila, Mexico at the Instituto de Filología Hispánica for "intense studies" in Spanish.

I really didn't have the money to do this, so I thought of a plan to get the money. I talked with my friend. She agreed to let me rent a room from her for one school term. Her home was only a couple of blocks from my work. That would be convenient for me. Both of us would benefit from the extra cash. So it was that I moved in with her and saved the money for the study trip.

My friend told me that our pastor would "never" give me his blessing for such a trip. I was praying and explaining to her that I had the money saved and only wanted to go and study. It wasn't as though I was going to chase guys. I said my motives were pure. Still she said over and over again that I might as well forget it. She said she knew him, and he would say, "No way!"

A few weeks before my deposits and paperwork had to be in I told my pastor that I needed to discuss something with him. We talked and I said, "I want you to pray about it." He said, "Sister, I always pray." He gave me a date to speak with him again about it, and I went home to wait.

My friend and I had the same discussion over and over. She always said the same, "He will never agree to that. If you want to go, you might as well just go without his approval." I told her I couldn't do that. If I needed prayer while there, or if anything happened to me while on the trip, he would be the one who would be expected to handle all the arrangements or offer up the prayers. It was important that he feel good about me and what I was doing.

One night at a prayer meeting I poured out my heart to God. I was so tired of being tormented over this issue. I finally I told the Lord that whatever his answer or however it worked out would be alright. I was tired of carrying this load.

One of our young ladies of the church was going on a mission trip and was saving her money for that. I told the Lord that if the pastor came back with a "no way" answer, I would give my money to her and forget about the trip. I also told my friend after the prayer meeting that I didn't know how it would work out, but I felt good about it. However it worked out, it would be alright. I felt "light" as we left the church and went home.

The appointment time rolled around. I was all prepared to give the pastor the same talk I had given to my friend. I met with him and said, "Have you prayed?" He said, "Sister, I always pray." I said, "You know what I mean." He smiled and said, "I think you have matured enough in the Lord to make that decision yourself." I thanked him, and I knew my answer. I was going on the study trip!

I made the trip and kept in touch with friends and family at home while there. It felt good to be able to share details of my trip with my pastor and his wife and know they were praying for me while I was away. We were both able to feel good about my trip.

When I returned, they had found me a nice little apartment to move into and were waiting to take me to see it and decide if it would be appropriate. It was near my work and rented for a reasonable amount. That is where I lived for the following school year.

> *"Behold, how good and how pleasant it is for brethren to dwell together in* **unity***!"*
>
> *"...for* **there** *God commands the blessing."* (Psalm 133: 1 and 3)

Treats for a Friend
and Her Boys

Sometimes God blesses us by allowing us to be a tool in His hands. During the years I worked at the grocery store, I was given a number of opportunities to be used this way. There were various reasons and different sources, but I was given a number of gifts to use to help others.

My new best friend from church had two sons. One was around 15 years old and the other around 10. One day the 15-year-old had a serious talk with his struggling, single mom about the fact that they seldom had desserts or other special treats. She reminded him that God had always met their needs and they should be thankful. She thought of his comments later and grieved over the truth of the statements he had made. She decided to pray about this matter. She wanted her kid to see that God would provide even those kinds of things.

I didn't have a lot, but I was an adult and could handle it. I was thankful just to be free of the worries of divorce and a bad marriage. It was enough. I was also thankful to be making new friends.

Suddenly at my work I started to get all sorts of little gifts. I got a whole box of Moon Pies which a salesman passed to my boss who passed them to me. Later, he gave me a half gallon of ice cream. Still later, he gave me a charcoal grill. I didn't want any of those items and passed them on to my friend and her boys.

If I had only money for a couple of orders of fries and a couple of soft drinks from a drive-through restaurant, I would invite the friend and the boys and we would share. After all, it wasn't any fun to eat alone.

Sometimes for Christmas or birthdays I could give sample-size cologne or some small gift to brighten the holiday a little. It was my joy to give.

I never knew about the talk and the prayers until after this all took place. She had never talked with me about wanting to see that God would provide those things.

After the boys were grown up, once she confided to me that her youngest was struggling financially. I had no extra money to give at the time. I prayed for him and his needs. I got out of my car on a parking lot shortly thereafter and saw bills folded together on the pavement. I didn't see anyone they might have belonged to, so I put them into my purse.

There were around twelve dollars in that little wad of cash. I felt sorry for the person who had lost the money but was thankful that God had provided help for Mil's son, and he was the one who got it.

While I waited for a full-time job, I got a very part-time one. It was only a day or two per week. I gave out food samples in grocery stores in the Dallas and Fort Worth areas. I was allowed to take the left over samples home at the end of the day. I actually didn't want them for myself, but my friend and the boys could use them. When my full-time job came through, she applied for and got the part-time job I had been doing. She had a job in downtown Dallas but needed the extra cash the part-time job would provide until she got a raise at her work. The small income from the part-time helped them get through the lean times.

> ...**all things** *work together for* **good** *to those who love God...* (Romans 8:28)

Race to the Door

My niece lived with me for a few years off and on after high school. She and I got along well and could work together pretty well. We worked out a plan to pay the bills and got an apartment large enough for both of us.

One thing that made our relationship work out was that each of us wanted to live for God. Every part of our existence centered on the Lord and church activities.

One Sunday night we came into the parking lot at our apartment complex and parked the car. I noticed a car parked two or three cars over with a few guys in it. I mentioned to her that they were there. I had a feeling about the situation. We had to walk toward their car and then turn toward our apartment. Just as we turned toward our apartment in front of their car, they started getting out. I whispered, "Hurry!", and we did! I already had the correct key in my hand and quickly opened the door and we went inside and locked it just as we heard footsteps close behind us. I told her that I was pretty sure they were up to no good.

A few nights later, she and I were at home for the night and already in bed. My bedroom was near the parking lot. I was not yet asleep. I heard a car pull into the parking spaces and someone close a car door. Suddenly, a woman let out a few screams and there was a scuffling commotion that followed.

Right away police cars came into the fray. I watched the blue lights flashing outside for a while, and then I drifted into a restless sleep.

The next morning, we heard what happened. A girl came in just as we had a few nights before. She was attacked and her purse snatched by someone who had been waiting on the parking lot.

I am thankful for that little nudge from the Spirit of God that warns us of problems. I would say discerning of spirits just when we need it.

The Boyfriend

I noticed while my niece was living with me that she rarely went out. There just weren't any young men her age really in the church. She went out a few times with people she met elsewhere, but when they saw she meant business about living for God, two or three dates and it was over.

On an extremely cold winter night, we were in the kitchen/dining room with the oven on just to keep warm. I looked at my little blond-haired, blue-eyed niece and felt very sorry for her. I said, "…I am an old woman (37 or 38), and I'm kinda used to sitting home alone all the time. You are young, and it's not even normal for you to be doing that. You should be going out with friends, dating, having fun. I am going to pray that God will send you someone in the church to date. I don't care if you marry him or not, but someone to go out with." She said, "Well, I wish you would." I did pray, starting that very night.

About a month after that, we walked into church one night and there was a visiting young man about her age. I sized him up because I was looking for my answer. After church was over, the pastor called my niece up to introduce her to our guest. I asked her on our way home what she thought of him and said, "Maybe he is my answer." She thought he was alright but just visiting and might not come back. After all, he was living across town so was likely to attend church over there.

He did come back, and when we would gather to talk after church, he seemed interested in my niece.

We were preparing to move from the apartment to a duplex next door to some church friends. I had a couple of volunteers (boys from church, but not boyfriend material☺) who were planning to help us move. The new guy told us he would help. We said we had it covered. He insisted, so we said okay. (It was amazing all the help I had getting things done when she lived with me.)

We made our move and settled in, and still he came to church. I guess we were a little surprised because he was driving from the other side of town.

As we left the church parking lot one night, I asked her what she thought of the new guy. She said that he was alright but he was engaged. I said, "He doesn't love the girl." She said, "How can you say that!?!? He's engaged!" I said, "People who are in love spend every moment possible with the person they love. He hasn't gone back home even once since he has been here. He seems to want to be around you a lot, and I think he is interested in you."

We would sometimes have snacks at our place and have church people over after church. He always came. I could see that his interest in her was growing.

One weekend he told us he was going home for the weekend and would not be back in time for church on Sunday. She could not hide her disappointment. On his way back, he called to ask if he could drop by our apartment for a while. It was after church and relatively late, but I said it was okay. He came in and sat in our living room with me present. I noticed that he was more serious than usual. Finally, he explained that he and his girlfriend had broken their engagement. I exchanged my I-told-you-so look with my niece. After a while he left.

They were an "item" from that point. He came to our side of town a lot after that. I learned, first hand, the feelings that mothers must have when their daughters are out. I could not sleep until she was not just in, but in bed. If the chatting in the living room lasted a bit late, I would finally get to the point of calling to her, "… I have to work tomorrow." Soon after, I would hear him leave, and then I could go to sleep. I never intended to take on the role of parent. It just happened. I can't say I liked that part. Besides, this kid came to me full-grown!

But, she had a boyfriend. My prayers had been answered. Marriage to him was not necessarily my dream for her, but in the next year she became a bride.

Thank God! My child rearing duties were over!

♫ Da, da, da, dum,
　　　Da, da, da, dum,
　　　　　　Da, da, da, da, dah, da, da, da, dum! ♫

Good job, Jesus!

Pastor and Sister Green

Coming to Texas from where I divorced in Arkansas, I had little faith in anybody. I thought it would be best to be in a really big church where I could get lost in the crowd. I wanted to ignore and be ignored, I thought. So-o-o, Jesus put me in a little church. Little churches I had seen in the past were basically petty, gossipy, way less than examples of righteousness.

I visited Christian Tabernacle where Warren Green was the pastor. I didn't expect to stay, but service after service I went back. Just a few services after I arrived in June of 1976, a healing took place in a service. A brother had some problem with his arm and couldn't raise it above a certain level. He was healed instantly in the service and raised his arms high over his head. I was blessed to see that. I would soon find out that this little church had frequent events like that. What the church lacked in size, it more than made up for in closeness to God. Pastor Green spoke with authority and boldness in the name of Jesus. Faith was "catching" at this church. People got the Holy Ghost in Sunday morning Sunday school! Pastor Green never hesitated to interrupt a lesson or service if he felt God leading him to do that. I liked this church. That surprised me. I wasn't just looking for miracles, but I saw a lot of them and began to realize that God never changes. He worked miracles in the past and still will.

In one service, Pastor Green announced to us that he saw a flag-draped casket as he sat on the platform. He said the flag wasn't an American flag or didn't seem to be. We prayed about it, especially for our military and family members with military connections. The service was finished and we went home. Before the next service, I heard on the news of the death of the Chinese leader, Mao Zedong. I immediately thought, "There is Brother Green's vision." He never called it a vision. That is my word for it. He just stated what he saw.

On another occasion, he told the congregation that he saw, as he sat on the platform in service, two circles of light that were broken. He said when he thought of circles, he thought of family circles. We prayed for our families. During that week, we heard of a local pastor's family's fatal accident. His wife had been on a street in Dallas with her two children in the car with her. She was stopped at a traffic signal and her car was hit from behind by someone fleeing from police, and it burst into flames. She and her infant son were killed. A service station attendant who saw the wreck rushed to the car and pulled the little girl to safety. Again, I knew when I heard of this wreck on the news that it was our pastor's vision.

> *That confirmeth the word of his servant, and performeth the counsel of his messengers; (Isaiah 44:26)*

Once, Pastor Green interrupted service to have us pray for all our families with military connections. He had seen the barrel of a rifle. We prayed. A few days later a former church member heard a commotion in his driveway near his vehicle. He stepped out on his porch to check it out and was shot dead by the car thieves.

Pastor Green never made a lot of noise about those miraculous occurrences. I would see him and his wife weeping and praying fervently for all of the little "sheep" of their pasture. It was in their church that I learned to pray more than five minute prayers. I learned to just lay it all out before God and expect answers to all that was laid out. Thank God for these fine role models. I have indeed been blessed to know them.

Pastor Green told me once, concerning the visions, that he just wished he would know who was involved so he could warn them before the events happened. I told him that I understood, but most people wouldn't believe him if he did.

> ...Nevertheless when the Son of man cometh, shall
> he find **faith** on the earth? (Luke 18:8)

I can say that the goal of that strong, little church was not "miracles". People were just focused on serving, worshipping God, and seeing souls saved. Miracles were just part of it. There were healings too numerous to tell. God would many times show Pastor Green what was wrong with the person before he prayed for them. That was fine if one was not sinning, but if one was, God would sometimes show him that too. He preached a sermon once called "Good Ole Repentance". That message was good for the guilty to hear. They came to appreciate the wonderful forgiveness of God in their lives.

I thank God for having had the privilege of learning from Pastor and Sister Green, my parents in the Lord.

Rio Grande Valley

Answer on a Bicycle

Who would think that God would send your answer on a bicycle? Well, that is just what happened when I lived in The Valley. Church services were held in a small trailer-sized portable building when I moved there. The church had started a building project, but it was not progressing very fast. We prayed and waited on God.

We started having work nights and all of our small flock would gather to do what we could on the building project. Money was not very plentiful, and our skills in building were lacking, to say the least. We stripped varnish from our old pews and got them ready to recover and refinish. The men worked inside the building and on water lines, etc., outside. It was getting there, but slowly.

One day as the men worked inside the new building, a man rode up on a bicycle and stopped to see what was going on. He came inside to look around. He pointed out some problem area to the pastor and was told to feel free to fix it if he thought he could. He did, and he did. He was told that we were not able to pay him much if anything. He kept coming and working. It turned out that he had a lot of experience in carpentry, and he was very skilled in many other areas of construction.

He soon started attending our church services, was baptized in Jesus' name, and filled with the Holy Spirit. He continued to attend church and to build. Soon he was a leader. He directed the men in building, plumbing, and electrical work. He directed the women in varnishing and covering the pews. He had a savings account somewhere in a bank and withdrew it all and gave it to the church for the building program.

I only lived in The Valley for three years, but our new building was finished before I left there. I got to attend a number of services in it before I moved.

I never heard what became of the bicycle man whose name I cannot recall, but I sincerely hope and pray that he is still walking on with Jesus and has been mightily blessed. He certainly was a blessing to us and to the work of God.

Fasting and Ford Cars

Like for most people, fasting has not been easy for me, but I like the results. Most times I fast for a day or two. But, one time I fasted for three whole days. For me, it was a lot! Our pastor had asked us to fast. I knew it was a way to humble ourselves and seek God for the release of souls from the bondage of sin. I had no particular person in mind. Most of my friends were already in church.

As I ended the fast, I walked to the group of mailboxes at my small apartment complex and stood looking at a few pieces of mail that I had received. A young man approached and made a comment about his troubles. I listened and he continued to talk. He said that he had checked himself into the hospital the previous year. I had seen this guy from my window as he came and went from his apartment a couple of doors down from mine. He looked like he had it all together. He was young, nice-looking, drove a nice car, and appeared happy. I just listened as he continued to talk. When he stopped, I asked if he had tried God. I told him where I attended church and that we were having special services but it was "rest night". He said, "If you will come and knock on my door I'll go with you next time."

I knocked on his door the next service night. He seemed to have forgotten the promise, but he quickly changed clothes and went with me.

I felt good about the service. The evangelist was young and had kept his messages positive. This fellow needed to see light at the end of his tunnel of despair. He was afraid that if he had to go in the hospital again it would have an effect on his job at a large car company. He was desperate.

I sat cringing through the message as the evangelist preached against about every sin in The Book. He was totally a different character that night. I could hardly believe the drastic change. The message went on and on with the same negative tones. Finally, I prayed in my mind, "God, you knew before he came what would be preached. Have Your way. I can't do anything. It is all up to You."

After church, we drove to a fast food place for a soft drink, and I asked him what he thought of the service. He said, "If I get in your church, I can't even have a beer with my dad and brothers." I said, "Well, you could still visit with them. Just have a Coke." He said, "Just suppose I drove a beer truck. I would have to quit my job." I said, "You don't drive a beer truck; but if you did, God would provide for your needs, perhaps with an even better job." We finished our drinks and conversation and went home. I could tell he was at one of those crossroads everybody faces sooner or later.

He never went to church again while I lived there. A few weeks later I moved back to Dallas. I gave the church men his address and work information and prayed that God would help him get deliverance and be saved.

> One plants, another waters, but **God** gives the
> increase. (I Cor. 3:6-7)

Kid on a Skateboard

Health issues had my attention just before I moved back to Dallas for four more years. I was troubled and couldn't seem to clear my thoughts.

I got in my little red Camaro to go somewhere one afternoon. I approached an intersection a few blocks from home and saw a boy about 12 years old riding his skateboard in the street. I thought about the danger involved and slowed to a very slow speed as I turned the corner and headed for the next. The next sign was a yield sign because the street merged into a busier city street at about a 45° angle. I was slowing to a stop and looking left for traffic before entering the street. As I looked back, out of nowhere came a boy on a skateboard. He hit the right front of my car, slid down the hood, and ended up under the car as I stopped. Had I not been stopping already, I would not have been able to stop.

I had the presence of mind to put the car in park and turn off the key. I was so frightened and in shock that I just sat there for a minute trying to absorb what had just happened. I couldn't see a bit of the child's body. He was totally under the front of my car. I hadn't felt the wheel roll over him, but I knew he must be injured. He had hit really hard just in front of my windshield, slid the full length of the hood, and then went out of sight under the car.

He crawled slowly out and started to try to get to his feet. He staggered to the curb holding his chest and gasping for breath. I could see bruises and scratches that were bleeding. I managed to get out of the car when I saw he wasn't dead. I covered my mouth and face with my hands and was shaking my head "no" as I made my way in his direction. He still sat on the curb gasping for air.

There had been a car right behind me as I approached the yield sign. The man and lady in the car had seen the whole thing. The lady came up to me by the time I got to the middle of my back bumper and bear-hugged me. She kept saying that he was going to be alright, but I had heard of people who were injured internally who later died. I was afraid it would happen to him.

The man called the police and then asked the boy if he was okay. The kid was breathing by then. That was a plus. I still didn't understand the blood and bruises. What on or under my car could have caused that?

The policeman came, and the kid I had seen at the other corner returned to where we were. The policeman interviewed the couple who had witnessed the incident. They had honked their horn when they saw him lose control. I heard it but thought they were trying to get me to hurry out of their way. They explained that I was stopping and looking left for traffic and the boy came off a parking lot on the right and down the three-foot embankment. He lost control of his skateboard and crashed directly into my car. The other skateboarder explained to the officer that the bruises and bleeding were caused by a wreck they had with a brick wall earlier in the day.

After a stern lecture, the officer made them get into his patrol car with their skateboards so he could take them home and talk with their parents. He advised me to pull my car to the parking lot and try to calm myself a little before driving. I was happy to follow his advice. Instead of going wherever I had been going, I just went home. I thought that the health problems were bad enough, but things could have gotten a lot worse. Thank God the kid only had the breath knocked out of him when he hit me. He could have easily been killed.

I lectured my second grade the next week about trying to be "Evel Knievel" riding skateboards on city streets and parking lots. We also had simplified math lessons about traveling speeds, weights of vehicles, and "stopping on a dime". I made it an annual lecture to future classes for a few years after it was over.

Raining Inside, Rocking Outside

Pastor and Sister Green came to The Valley to visit our new church and me. They were to preach for us a few services while there. I looked forward to their visit, and I was excited that they were staying with me.

I had heard older people tell stories of going to church in "olden days" and having rocks thrown at the church or brush arbor. I thought it was just some barbaric happening of yesteryear. But, during one service in our new building, while Brother Green preached and the Spirit of the Lord rained down inside, I heard rocks hitting the roof outside. I guess someone must have been listening and didn't like what they heard. Maybe the message put them under conviction! The service went on without missing a beat, and all was well, at least at church.

At home, it was maybe a little too well—done, that is. I had put a roast on to cook and estimated the time service would be over and we would get home for lunch. Pastor Green held a little longer than I had guessed. We arrived at my townhouse to a burned roast! I wasn't about to waste a good roast. I tried to trim away the burned side and served it anyway.

Is it any wonder that I earned the reputation of not being the best cook in the world? They say, "The way to a man's heart is through his stomach." If that is true, no wonder I never married again!

Neither Pastor nor Sister Green complained about the burned roast, or about having to sleep on flip chairs for a bed. However, they must have prayed. Now I have a real bed in my guest bedroom and a stove with a timer that shuts the oven off when the roast is ready.

A Bride for Brother Noe

I met a man at church in The Valley who was blind. He and I became good friends. It all started when his sister needed to be somewhere else at the same time he needed to be at a singles meeting. She called me to ask if he could ride with me if she delivered him to my apartment. I agreed to her plan, and I felt a little nervous as I waited for their arrival. I didn't know if I should help him to the car or he could get there independently. When she rang the doorbell, I said I was ready and locked my door. She turned and left before I could figure out how to handle the situation. I just said we should go and headed to the car, leaving him to fend for himself. I did open his car door and remove a box of tissues from the seat. We arrived at our destination and I spotted a couple of church guys arriving also. I left them to get him inside and was glad they rescued me. Of the two of us, I think I was the more helpless.

That little trip started a friendship that goes on even now. We began talking regularly by phone. I was comfortable with that. I learned that he had lost his vision in a hunting accident when he was a teen. He had gone through surgeries but never regained his vision. He attended a school for the blind and developed many skills and worked at the hospital. He was well able to do most things on his own by the time I met him.

I enjoyed being his eyes for some things. For example, talking on the phone with him one day, I described ladies clothing styles and he was very surprised. Long, loose-fitting knits were "in". All those years before when he was last able to see, girls were wearing mini-skirts and boots.

We talked about church and both loved living for God. He told me one day that he hoped to someday have a wife. I told him I was sure God had someone for him. He knew a girl from his school, but she wasn't in church. The pastor had advised him against getting involved with her.

He called me another day and said he had met a nice lady where he worked and was planning to invite her to church. He hoped I would meet her. She came, and I greeted her briefly. He called when I got home to ask what I thought of her. I told him she seemed nice, but I only saw her for a minute. He said he would ask her back, and he wanted me to really look her over and tell him what I thought. He said the hospital guys didn't talk about her as they did other girls, and that was a good thing.

She came to church again, and I spent more time trying to get to know her. I was ready for his call that afternoon. I told him she was beautiful, intelligent, and seemed to enjoy the church service.

They continued to date and were married just after I left The Valley. I missed the wedding!!! A friend sent me the newspaper clipping. They have now been married long enough to have two beautiful grown-up daughters. His sweet family faithfully serves the Lord and is a great blessing to the work of God.

I am glad God worked it out so well. It would have been a great disappointment to me if my brother Noe's dream of marriage and a family had not come true. I love them so much. We still e-mail or call each other at least a few times each year.

The family of God is such a special blessing.

Moving On

Surgery

I returned from The Valley and took the second job that I was offered when I first started teaching in Texas. I had been diagnosed with fibroid tumors while in The Valley, but I really didn't want to be down there for their treatment. I thought that with my pastor to pray for my healing maybe they would just dry up and I wouldn't need surgery. I made my annual doctor visits and they did not go away. They became so large that I started having breathing difficulty when I slept at night. I still was not told to get surgery until a doctor visit when I told my doctor that I could feel the lump high up at my waistline or higher. He checked that out and sent me for a sonogram that day. He said I needed immediate surgery before it possibly ruptured and became an emergency surgery. He seemed a bit disgruntled when I did not agree to that right away. I waited about another month before calling to tell him I would agree to surgery. By the time I had the surgery, it was three or four months later.

The tumor was huge for a little, barely-hundred-pound woman. The doctor measured with his hands to show me how big it was. He couldn't believe I had no great pain with it. I don't know why God chose not to heal that. Or, maybe He did heal it. It wasn't cancerous! He just didn't do it in the way I had envisioned. Maybe a doctor needed to see the workings of God.

I had banked my blood for the surgery, but the doctor said it wasn't needed because I probably didn't lose more than "a tablespoon of blood". I remember waking up talking to the Lord in another language than my native English. Maybe the doctor needed to witness that. I know my pastor's daughter and I had the same doctor. She had talked to him about the Lord and our beliefs. Perhaps I was confirmation of her words to him.

Pastor and Sister Green took me to their home and took care of me through the first week after surgery. What caring, precious people! Praise God! I survived and felt better than I had in a long time—once I got over the surgery. Sister Green's good cooking and care helped speed my recovery.

Christmas Eve on Ice

Ah-h-h! Christmas vacation at last! It was Christmas Eve and in seven hours I would be at Mom's with the whole family. I wondered what gifts I would get. I wondered if things had changed much since I was home last time. ...couldn't wait for some of Mom's turkey and dressing!

The streets were clear in Texas as I drove I-30 toward Arkansas. The sun was shining, and I felt good! It was noon and the recent snow had melted off the roads. I drove, thought, and switched from station to station on the radio catching up on, and laughing at, the latest crazy songs that I haven't had time to hear.

Suddenly, I noticed ice on the road and traffic slowing to a crawl. Maybe I should go back. No, I would keep going. The sun should melt this off soon. They were expecting me.

It was beginning to get dark. I saw a sea of red taillights ahead. I wondered what happened. I lined up with the rest of the taillights, and like everyone else, I was on a solid sheet of ice. No one was going anywhere. I waited...and waited. Still we were not moving. I turned my motor and lights off and sat there, and sat there, and sat there. Still we went nowhere. I could see through the night that trucks and cars were off in the median ahead. Maybe when they got them out we would move again.

A trucker offered to walk over the hill to an all-night truck stop/restaurant and get me a snack. I thanked him and said that I had snacks in the car. I decided that this would be my very first time to spend Christmas Eve on ice sharing my snacks with truckers and everyone else from everywhere else. People were out of their cars talking, looking, getting angry, playing on the ice, and trying to find a place to use the restroom.

At last, we saw the lights beginning to move. I carefully moved with them, sometimes hanging my tires off the pavement on one side for traction. Many tense hours later, I arrived at Mom's house. It was 1:30 in the morning Christmas Day. Mom hadn't slept, but she was still happy to see me.

Nobody Notices

I had moved back to the Dallas area from The Valley. I felt like I was just here temporarily. I even mentioned that to my pastor. I knew I had health issues that needed to be watched and wanted to be near people I knew and loved while I waited to see how it would all play out.

I lived for God and loved Him, but probably because I was not healed of my health problems, didn't know if He really knew where I was. I just kept on living for Him and was not thinking of giving up, but I felt like I wasn't getting anything done for God. I hoped for things to turn around for me, whatever that meant.

One Sunday on my way home from the morning church service, I thought as I drove. "I am doing this, but nobody even sees enough of God in me to know that I live for Him. All the people I have invited to church are not attending now. Even those who were baptized and filled with the Holy Ghost are not attending church now."

Just at about that point in my negative review, I came to a shopping center that had a grocery store. I needed an item or two, so I whipped into a parking place and went into the store. I grabbed my basket and started down an aisle. A man came up to me and said, "You're a Christian, aren't you?" After I almost dropped my teeth from shock, so to speak, I replied that I was. He went on to say that he could tell. He told me where he went to church and I told him where I attended. He made a few more comments about recognizing the people of God and then moved on. I also finished my shopping and started home.

As I got into my car, I don't think I could have heard God's voice any more clearly if He had spoken audibly to me! It was as if He said, "I know exactly where you are and so do people. They also know who you are—a child of Mine. I am working in your life. **Trust Me.**

Master of the Wind

On one of my trips home to Arkansas from Texas, there came up one of those quick, dangerous storms. Mom is terrified of storms. She has been through a couple of tornadoes. That will give the bravest of people a healthy respect for the damage they can do.

She quickly decided that we must go to her storm shelter. I wasn't sure which I was more afraid of—the storm or the shelter. Anyway, we ran to the laundry room and started to open the back door to go into the carport but could see that it was blowing and raining too hard to even try it.

I stopped, grabbed Mom's hand, and whispered a quiet prayer asking God to calm the storm and protect us. Almost instantly the wind stopped. Mom looked surprised. We went back inside and watched the rain.

Texas Tumbleweed

West Texas Job

I was having an especially difficult year teaching. I felt that maybe it was time to move again. The surgery was over, and I had thought God had returned me to the Dallas area for that. I had a doctor here that I trusted. I did not have that in The Valley. Anyway, I told Pastor Green my thoughts. He said, "I think you should wait and pray about it for another school year. I did that. I was learning that "...in the multitude of counselors there is safety." *(Proverbs 11:14)*

After another year of teaching that was even more difficult, I took a trip to the mountains of Texas and studied at Sul Ross State University. I had placed applications there, just in case, and prayed them in. I had also told my principal at the school where I taught that if a job came through, I was gone!

A couple of weeks before school started, I was offered a job teaching gifted/talented half a day and third grade the other half. I submitted my resignation to my old school and accepted the new position.

I enjoyed living and working there better than any place I have ever lived. I was blessed of God to be there for eight years and thought I would live there the rest of my life. God had other plans, or I should say better plans.

*And we know that **all** things work together for **good**
to them that love God, to them who are the called
according to His purpose. (Romans 8:28)*

I have learned to accept the moves that the Lord brings to me
with a thankful heart. I have been blessed to meet friends that
I wouldn't have met except for the relocations. I can't imagine
life without them. Many of them are church friends, and it is
good to know I can keep them for eternity. I hope I have been
a blessing to them, too.

Spots Healed

A friend had a black-looking raised lump just above her lip. She said it felt itchy and started to bother her more as time passed. She had a lot of faith because we would go to our pastor many times and he would pray for us and God would heal us. She had prayer for this spot, but it wasn't leaving. She told me that she decided that every time she noticed it she was going to touch it with a finger and thank God for healing it. The spot went totally away! Praise God!

I had a brown spot on the side of my face, and it started giving me trouble. I thought, "God is no respecter of persons. If He did that for her, He will do it for me." I did the same thing she did, and He healed my spot too! I testified about it in church.

There was another spot on my face, but it wasn't troubling me, so I didn't get prayer for it. I had that one for about as long as I could remember and thought it was probably something like a birthmark. I guessed it would go with me to my grave.

Sometime after the first healing, I walked into the church one night just as Pastor Green and Sister Green walked in. Brother Green said, "I need to pray for you." I had no clue for what. He touched the spot on my face and prayed. Soon after, it was totally gone! Again, to God be the glory!

It is such a blessing to have a pastor who is in tune with God and concerned for the flock over which God has placed him as an under-shepherd.

Texas Dust Storm

Many times when I worked in West Texas I was sent to the Midland/Odessa area for workshops. I also had doctor appointments there quite a bit. Sometimes I would go just to stock up on supplies to last for several months. I don't remember why I was there on this particular trip, but as I started to leave Midland to return home, I noticed a muted pink color of dust in the air. Just outside of Odessa, the winds really picked up and the dust increased. It started to sprinkle a few drops of rain. I thought that was a good thing. Maybe there would be a downpour and wash the dust out of the air. There wasn't. It rained only enough to cause muddy streaks on my windshield, and then stopped.

I drove on. The farther I drove toward Pecos, the harder the wind blew and the more dust was in the storm. I flipped on the radio for a weather report. The announcer said the winds were clocked at 120 miles per hour on Guadalupe Peak and some trucks had been blown off the highway. I was already in the big middle of it by then and just drove on. Traffic on I-20 was moving at a crawl – around 15 or 20 miles per hour. There were two reasons: one was the extreme wind and the other was that we couldn't see more than a white stripe or two ahead of us. At least we were all traveling in the same direction and at a very slow speed, so if there were an accident, maybe it wouldn't be too bad.

I was driving a few car lengths behind two eighteen wheelers. One was in the left lane and the other in the right. The one in the left lane apparently was not loaded and his trailer leaned dangerously to the left. He stayed about a trailer-length behind the one in the right lane which seemed to offer him a bit of protection from the force of the wind. The one in the right lane must have had a heavy load and seemed to be weathering the storm fairly well. I knew there was no reason to want around them. None of us were going anywhere fast, and they were giving me some protection as well.

After listening to the weather report, I wished I had checked into a motel in Midland for the night!

It had been dark for a while by the time I neared Pecos. I thought that I would exit at the State Police Headquarters and ask if they thought I could make it to through the mountains. If not, maybe I could get a motel room for the night. I had no cell phone at that time and couldn't call to ask.

I took the exit but saw nobody out at the headquarters. I was afraid to even try to open my car door, much less go into the building. I decided to just keep moving slowly along and hope and pray for the best.

I headed toward Balmorhea from Pecos directly at a right angle to the wind. I could hear the sand as it blasted the right side of my car. Road signs were being flattened to the ground as I went along. I worried that the drivers in the small amount of traffic would not be able to see any better than I could and we would collide. I would see taillights or headlights just seconds ahead of me. I wondered, "Who are these silly people out on a night like this, and what are their lame excuses?" On we went. I thought that anything might be blowing across the fields through the night and I wouldn't be able to see it. I passed a store that sat near the road and could vaguely see by the store lights that the large awning across the front had been partially blown down. I pressed on. It was somewhat like driving through heavy fog as far as visibility was concerned – a real strain on the eyes.

I prayed that Jesus would get me safely to my little dog who was home alone. The thought crossed my mind that if I was blown into the flat field, it would be hours and hours before anyone would even find me. I crept on. Just before Balmorhea, suddenly, all stopped and I was under clear, star-lit skies.

The next day at school I told my coworkers that I truly knew the meaning of "coming in on a wing and a prayer", or maybe a bunch of prayers.

As I picked up my mail at the post office that day, I mentioned my ordeal to the postmaster. He said he too had been out there in the storm between Balmorhea and Pecos. Now I knew at least one other silly who was out there with me that night!

Those who were in my small town during the storm said that winds were clocked at 80 miles per hour in front of our high school.

A storage building had been blown into the street in front of my trailer, but my trailer was still intact. My puppy was obviously shaken but safe. He was always nervous in stormy weather after that.

We had much for which to be thankful. I was glad my Lord was on board with me that night!

Muffi's Healing

*...sparrows...**one of them** shall not fall on the ground without your Father.*
*But the very **hairs of your head are all numbered**. (Matt. 10: 29-30)*

I have never had a child or been able to adopt one. In 1990, I finally decided with a little urging from a friend, to get a puppy. That is when little Muffi came to live at my house. He was a darling little dog and I wondered, after getting him, why I hadn't done that long before. He brought hours of fun and joy to our house.

When he was about seven years old, we planned a trip to Arkansas from Texas to visit my parents. Muff hated to ride in the car, so I took him to the vet and got tranquilizers for him to take on the thousand-mile trip. He was showing signs of not feeling well before we left home, but I hoped he would be better before we got to Mom and Dad's. He was not. He seemed to grow worse with each new day. On a Friday, I panicked when I got up for the day and discovered that his eyes were rolling back and he had wet his bed. I called a local vet who would see him and headed to her office as fast as I dared drive.

Right away the vet realized he was extremely ill and told me I would have to leave him at the clinic. Muff could not even stand up by that time. The vet said I could come to visit him on Saturday if he made it through the night.

I left the office with a heavy heart. I told the Lord that he was all I had and asked Him to allow me to keep him if it could be His will. I told Him to please let us get back to Texas where I could bury him at home if he had to die.

Later that day, I drove to my brother's house. He and his wife were out in their back yard working on playground equipment. They are praying people, so I interfered with their work while I poured my story out to them. About dusk, I took my lonely, miserable self back to Mom and Dad's. My night was very restless. I could hardly wait to return to the vet's office the next day.

Upon my arrival there the next morning, I entered and sat a couple of chairs to the left of the entrance door. Other people were there, and I knew I would probably have to wait until they were all processed out because the office closed at noon for the weekend. All the people left but me, and I waited. The vet came out and brought Muffi out for me to hold. She told me she could not make me any promises. I sat with his limp little body draped across my arms and cried. Suddenly the door opened and a lady entered the office. She walked to the chair beside me and sat down, bypassing the rest of the empty chairs. She said, "Is your little dog sick?" I replied with a simple "nod yes" and nothing more. I thought it a strange question since she could see that he was. Anyway, I decided that I would ask the doctor to let me take him home with me. I felt he would feel better near me than lying in a cage and only being checked every few hours. The lady left and we never saw her again. I wondered later if she might have been an angel since she apparently had no business to do there.

The vet did allow me to take Muff with me to Mom's house and sent his medicine with us. She said to bring him back on Monday morning first thing if he made it that long. I sat all the rest of the day at Mom's with him limp in my arms. I cried and waited. Now and then I would take him out and support his body so he could use the bathroom.

Just before dark, my brother and his wife came over to visit. By then my arms were so tired, and I had finally placed Muff on a pad in his pet taxi next to the sofa where I was sitting. When they came into the room and sat down, Muff jumped up and ran to my sister-in-law for sympathy. His little legs were sliding out from under him as he went. She made a fuss over him and his sickness. He went to my brother who did likewise. He began to get stronger from then on. I have no doubt that they had been praying for him too.

By Monday he was eating, playing, and fit as could be. We went back to the vet. She said, "Put him down on the floor." I told her he was much better and would probably run away from us. She acted doubtful and told me to put him down anyway because there was no place for him to go but down the hall. I placed him on the floor and he shot out of the exam room and down the hall to the office. She looked really surprised!

We paid our vet bill and, after visiting a few more days, returned to Texas. Muffi lived to be 14 ½ year old. I believe God healed him. **God is love.**

Black Ice

I traveled a couple of thousand miles round trip to visit my parents and family when I lived in West Texas. I would go half way and spend the night with my friend and make the rest of the trip the next day. I did the same thing in reverse returning home.

One Christmas vacation I saw that the weather was likely to get bad in Arkansas and left for home a little early. Things were fine all the way to Dallas. It was even okay the next morning as I left for the last leg of the trip home. My Muffi and I were driving and trying not to get sleepy by listening to the radio and eating snacks.

Just before Big Springs, the traffic started to slow a bit. Some moved fast, but others didn't. A light rain was falling by then. I slowed a little to allow for the rain and kept moving. Traffic went even slower. With a very slight sideways slide of the rear wheels of my car, I woke up to the fact that what looked like a wet blacktop was actually black ice. A few more miles ahead, the rain was freezing on my windshield wipers. I turned up the heat and flipped on the de-icing devices. I couldn't stop in the middle of nowhere.

We stopped at Big Springs for gasoline. The station attendant said, "Young lady, you need to get off the road and check into a motel somewhere. People traveling the other way on I-20 are saying that the same weather is also west of us." I thanked him for the advice but kept moving.

It was getting late by the time I reached Odessa, and I was afraid to risk going on in that kind of weather. It was bad enough here in the flat area. What would it be like in the mountains! We got a motel room in Odessa and spent the night. The TV weather channel was issuing all kinds of warnings. I was glad for a warm place to sleep for my little dog and me.

We got up a little late the next morning and started home. The sun was bright and I thought it would begin to melt the ice soon. About ten miles out of Odessa, there wasn't a bit of ice or snow on the road and all the roads were clear the rest of the way home. I was still glad we stopped for a good night's sleep rather than fighting our way that extra ten miles. Who knows what might have happened in those ten miles. It pays to follow those little, quiet leadings of the Holy Spirit.

A Friend's Job Miracles

A friend called me one night while I lived in the mountains to say that she was worried about losing her job. She had more or less been forced into retirement by the company where she worked and had landed this job with a used car dealership that had just opened. The pay wasn't great, but it paid the bills. The problem was that some of the employees were working some deals that the headquarters didn't know about. They were also getting caught up with and fired. She feared that the dealership would close and she would be out of work.

I told her she wasn't going to lose hers. We were going to pray. I reminded her that, when they were dealing with her, they were dealing with a child of God! I said God would defend and provide for her. I said He would either help her keep the job she had, or provide her a better one.

After everything blew up and the pieces settled to the ground again, everyone lost their job except the friend. Even the manager was fired, but my friend continued to work. The owner told her that he needed someone to field calls from customers and answer their questions. She went to work every day to an almost empty building. Only a bit of office equipment remained. Most days she said there was nothing to do but read.

She kept that job until God opened a better job for her with a popular telecommunications company. She remained there until she retired again. Isn't God good?

My sweet friend sings a song:

> ♫ I have never seen the righteous forsaken or His seed begging for bread.
>   …
>
> You may be down today, but help is on the way.
> Dark clouds may cover your sky, but He will answer you bye and bye.
> If you'll take one step, He'll take two,
> There is no limit to what God can do!
>
> And I've never seen the righteous forsaken, or His seed begging for bread. ♫

Days with Dad

September 1996, after years of heart problems and strokes, Dad was hospitalized again. I wasn't really surprised.

I dreamed that I was in a large church that was crowded with church people who were happily visiting with each other. There was Sister Verona Harris. Just inside the doors was Dad. I connected the two in my dream as both having passed away. Dad was wearing a carpenter's apron that was long over his overalls. He held a little dog, much like mine, wiggling out of the bib of his apron. He looked very happy, young, and walked with a spring in his step like he did when he was young. I walked toward him and said, "Well, are you going to give me a hug?" He behaved as though he couldn't see or hear me. It was as though he was looking through or past me. The dream was over.

I made my travel plans and went to see my dad. I remember praying as I sat in the CVICU. I read my New Testament that I carried with me. Mary said she knew her brother would live in the "last day" and even now Jesus was able to give him life. I felt that way about Dad.

He was in the hospital for about a week before he was dismissed to go home. This time we had him for a little while longer. I told some of my relatives that I didn't think he would make it another year.

Work and life went on, and I was sent to San Antonio to a week-long workshop in June of the next year. My brother called me to say that Dad wasn't doing well and he didn't know if he would make it or not. He was again in the hospital, and it didn't look good for him. I told him I would be there, but because it was Friday and the bank was closed until Monday, I would have to wait to leave until I could get travelers' checks.

I went to prayer that night in my usual place, sitting on an ottoman and leaning back across a chair in the living room of my trailer. I was pouring my prayers out to God for Dad, myself, my family, etc. I stopped praying and looked up into the semi darkened room lit only by a night light. I watched as a tiny spark of light, about a foot from the ceiling, blinked in the hallway leading from my bedroom to the kitchen. It blinked again, and again as it moved off to the right into the kitchen and never blinked again. I got up and turned on the kitchen light and looked for a source. I found none. I went on to bed. I waited until I could travel. I had thought maybe I would not get home to Dad in time. I wasn't sure I wanted to. I loved my daddy so much and wasn't sure I had the strength to see him die.

I did get to him and he was so happy to see me. He even seemed a little better for a few days. We fought our way through some treatment issues, but I could see that he was on the decline. It became a matter of waiting. My heart ached for him and for Mom who was worn out by being his full-time caregiver at the age of 73 years old. I feared losing them both at the same time. Her strength was about gone, and her nervous and emotional states were wrecked. I walked the hall in front of his room and prayed my concerns to my Jesus.

Just past midnight, July 14th, my dad passed away. I was with him at that moment. My face was pressed against his. My eyes and the nurse's eyes met silently across his bed, and I knew that he was gone.

My brother was in the room and so was Mom. There was a feeling of great peace. I believe the room was filled with angels and the Lord, if only I had been able to see them.

My dream and the twinkling light brought comfort to me during the following hours and days. God had given me about three and a half weeks with my dad, and he was awake and knew me. We communicated, though he couldn't speak clearly. I was glad God had given me the time with him.

It is hard to say goodbye,

♪♪...but there's a better home awaiting...♪♪

Daylight at Night

I was returning from Midland after going there for whatever reason, and as usual, it was after dark already. The night was overcast and quite dark. I drove homeward with my mind roving over hill and dell. I thought, "Hum, it looks like it is getting lighter outside instead of darker, but that is impossible." Slowly it grew much lighter. I could see the clouds overhead, the road ahead as far the eye could see, and out across the fields all around me. Because of the clouds, I could not see if there was a visible light source. However, I knew it had to be something big. There was a rippling effect to the light above the clouds as I stared out of my car windows. I drove on, and after a few minutes it was dark again. I did a little talking to myself, "Self", I said, "It will be best to just not mention this to anybody because they would never believe it. They would think you are totally crazy!"

The next day at school, one of my third grade boys said, "Last night I was looking out the window and I told my mom that it was getting daylight outside. She didn't believe me until she looked out." I told him that I believed him because I had been driving and had seen the same thing. This phenomenon covered at least 30 or 40 miles because the kid was in a town that far away from where I was.

It was later announced on a local news program that there had been numerous calls from people wanting to know what it was. Of course, they had only theories/maybe's. They no more knew what it was than I did.

Recalling, I wasn't afraid, just curious. Again, I was glad to have had the Master Driver, Jesus, on board with me.

> *...signs...*
> *...Men's hearts failing them for fear, and for looking after those things which are coming on the earth: for the powers of heaven shall be shaken.* (Luke 21:24-26)

Dental Infection

Have you ever had a dental infection? You don't want one!

I felt a slight throbbing under one of my bridges, but I thought I could surely put off the dentist until school was out. I did wait. I had a full-blown infection with body aches, chills, the works by the time the appointment rolled around the first Monday after school was out.

I got prayer at church that Sunday, but by my appointment was too sick to drive myself to it. A friend drove me and I arrived before lunch time. They started working on my teeth, gave me a lunch break, and worked some more. When I started shaking uncontrollably, they covered me with a blanket and continued. By the time they released me form the dental chair at around seven o'clock that night, they had done two root canals, numerous x-rays, and were sending me home with instructions: "No matter what, do not stop taking these antibiotics, even if you feel better."

My friend waited in the store with me. She wasn't too well herself, and I felt really awful to keep her out so late. The druggist had to clear my insurance. We waited and waited. Finally, I was exhausted and so sick I felt I couldn't stand it anymore. I was suddenly overwhelmingly weak. Tears were pouring from my eyes. People just stared. No one offered a place to sit or any kind of help. When I was wondering if they would ever get my insurance cleared, they finally gave me my meds. I told my friend that I could not take them on an empty stomach, so we stopped at a cafeteria and I ate a few bites and took my meds.

It was around midnight by the time I got home. I tried to talk my friend into staying the night. She had to go home so I was left alone to get through the night.

I felt horrible and propped myself up against pillows on the sofa to try to get a little rest. I had a lot of really strange feelings. Around 2:30 a.m., I knew I needed someone with me. I knew nobody who would come. I called a friend from church and she didn't want to drive the 25 miles in the night. I finally called the school secretary, a kind lady. Her husband answered the phone. I made my plea, and she got dressed and was at my door by around 3:00 a.m. She sat with me the rest of the night even though she had to work that day. She refused to leave until she had called the only doctor in town and arranged to get me worked in for an appointment. I insisted on taking a shower first. When I looked in the mirror, I was a ghastly pale color. She later described it as more blue or purple than "pale". She helped me dress for the doctor visit. I went to the appointment and she went to work.

The doctor checked me out and sent me home to continue with the antibiotics which "should have been given for several days before the dental work was done".

I took them all summer until a couple of weeks before I was to go back to work. I called the dentist and told him I had to quit taking them. They were making me feel horrible and I couldn't work feeling like that. I told him the offending tooth still felt the same and I wanted it pulled out. He said if I insisted on that I would have to sign a release. I insisted. This was one of the teeth on which he had done or tried to do a root canal, and I had already paid. I went back and he removed the tooth. He told me I was right about the tooth having to be removed. It was cracked all the way through the root. The infection was trapped between the parts of the cracked tooth and just kept coming back after antibiotics were out of my system.

My body was so full of antibiotics that wearing a wrist watch caused my skin to break out for several months after I had stopped seeing the dentist.

Had it not been for the protection of Almighty God, I do not think I would be writing this today. ---a very present help in time of trouble. I am thankful to Him for taking care of me.

In What-so-ever State I Am

Everybody Needs
Praying Grandparents

I could see that God was working on restoring my dad. It was not an instant thing, but line upon line, precept upon precept. I observed and tried not to push issues. God would work in His own time and way. I'll confess that sometimes that was hard.

Mom dreamed a bad dream about my divorced niece and her two precious little children. She was greatly troubled when she woke. She told my Dad about her dream and he had dreamed the same dream! Knowing the gravity of the situation, and trusting that it was a warning from God for that little family, Mom told Dad that she knew they couldn't do anything but pray. God could help. They prayed. When my niece came to visit them, Mom told her about their dreams, concerns, and prayers. She cautioned her to be careful.

My niece shared an apartment with another lady and sometimes left her children with the woman when she needed a sitter. She started to learn about some involvement the woman had with drugs. The little ones had even seen some of the goings on, but I guess the woman thought they were too little to know or talk about what was happening. My niece moved her children out so fast that they even left some of their belongings behind. She feared losing custody of her children if her x-husband found out about their exposure to such goings-on.

Later, the woman and some of her family were arrested on drug charges. Had my niece lived with her at the time, she and her little ones would have been in the big middle of that.

Thank God for praying grandparents!

Where Were You…?

I am sure you would finish the above question as everyone who experienced the event would. Where were you on 9/11?

I was on my way to work when I heard a news story that made me think, "Will these people never stop making these mistakes?" A plane had crashed into the World Trade Center.

I went on to work and taught an hour or more. In the middle of a class period, the teacher across from my classroom came to my door and beckoned me. That was unusual. I stepped to the door and pushed it almost closed to hear what she had to say. Her husband had called her and told her that the crash into the World Trade Center was a terrorist attack. He was watching the news.

We tensely went back to what we had been doing. A scripture came to my mind from a Bible study that I had done during the summer. It was very impacting when I read it; so much so, that I had read it to my mom with emphasis on the parts that stood out to me. The scripture ministered comfort to me now. Soon we received a call from the office informing us to keep this information from the students and just keep teaching. We would be updated as news came in. It was Grandparents' Day for the students, and we would try to continue as we always did unless we were forced to alter our plans.

Parents and grandparents came to eat with the kids, but they did a very good job of not saying anything about the news. We had a real turnout! I am sure most of them were thinking that they would rather take their little ones home, but everything stayed calm. Some of the fourth or fifth grade students had started to find out about it by the middle of the afternoon, but we managed to keep it quiet until dismissal time. I felt a bit like I was trying to hold my hand on the lid of a pressure cooker, but we got through it.

At the end of the day, my friend and I watched TV reports as people joined hands and jumped to their deaths from upper floors of buildings rather than die in the collapse or the flames. It was a numbing experience to see it unfold.

The next few days were eerie. I would walk outside to total silence. I lived in the Dallas area where at any given moment of the day or night you could normally walk out and hear traffic, multiple planes, and all kinds of city noises. Planes had been grounded, so there was nothing—total silence.

I knew by the next church service time why God had impressed the scripture so strongly on my mind during the summer. People at church that night were quiet, but I could hardly wait for testimony service! I planned to deliver to my sweet brothers and sisters what God had given to me. I felt like shouting!

> *Fear thou not; for **I** am with **thee**: be not dismayed; for **I am thy God**: **I** will strengthen thee; yea, **I** will help thee; yea, **I** will uphold thee with the right hand of my righteousness. (Isaiah 41:10)*

He is not just a god. He is The God! All power in heaven and on earth is in Him! I praise and worship this King of kings and Lord of lords! As my pastor used to say, "He's got this whole thing hanging out here on nothing. He has it all under control." Isn't it wonderful to know that kind of God?!

* * * * * * * * *

I want to put a word into this for our President at the time. He and his family handled the situation with great wisdom and dignity under extreme pressure. One thing that impressed me was their willingness to confess our nation's need of God's help. I don't know of anyone who would have done a better job. I was proud of them. "...honor to whom honor is due."

Gifts and Calling of God

I studied something in church that stuck with me. "For the gifts and calling of God are without repentance". (Romans 11:29). One view of this verse is that God gives you these "gifts and callings" and expects you to use them; and once He gives them to you, He never takes them back. You are an obedient child of His or a disobedient child of His, but the gifts were given to you and are still yours when you are living a pure and repented life. I believe that. This narrative will explain why.

My dad became offended and bitter after some disappointing church experiences. He got his eyes on the people of the church and off the Master. For a while, it was so bad that we would not even mention church or God to him for fear of setting off a tirade of harsh words. I grieved over it for years.

My move to Texas and study of the Bible with an excellent Bible teacher, Pastor Warren Green, opened my eyes to a few things I never knew before. One of those things was about the gifts and calling of God. I knew Dad had been used of God in his younger years but had gotten cold spiritually and everything changed.

Little-by-little he again started to tolerate talk about God and the things of God without "coming unglued". So, on one trip home, I talked in the living room with Mom about our Bible study on the gifts and calling of God. I knew he was listening from his bedroom, even though he made no comments.

A short time after our talk about God's gifts, my aunt and uncle visited Mom and Dad. This was Dad's sister and her husband, a Baptist/Nazarene preacher. They poured out their story of grief about not seeing or hearing from their son for a very long time. They didn't really even know if he was still alive. He had not made contact with his parents in years.

Daddy told them he was going to pray, and they would hear from him. He gave them a two or three-week window of time to expect to hear. He prayed, and they went back to their home.

Within the window of time Dad had given them, they showed up at Mom and Dad's with an extra person. It was their son! They all were thankful and had a nice visit with the young man.

God still works in our time, and the "gifts and calling of God are without repentance".

> O the depth of the riches both of the wisdom and
> knowledge of God!
> (Romans 11: 33)

Tug-of-war Healing

The year I retired from teaching, my last few days of school were filled with the usual end-of-school activities. Among those was a teacher tug-of-war. I always hated doing it. This school had it every year on Field Day. I was sometimes ridiculed because I didn't dress out, wear make-up, and cut my hair. So, to try to be part of the activities for my kids' sake, I wore a loose-fitting, long dress and participated. I was placed on a team opposite some real heavyweights. This would be a real battle.

Just prior to the tug-of-war, students had run relays on the gym floor and were sweaty and dirty. I am sure you already know where this is going. We took our positions and started to pull. Our cheerleaders (classes) were yelling their encouragement. We had barely started when my feet hit a wet spot on the floor and I took a big spill! One leg went straight out and the other bent under me in the other direction, almost like doing the splits. Two more people fell on top of me. I was in so much pain I just lay there for a couple of minutes. Of course, the audience laughed. Someone helped me to my feet, and someone else filled in for me so that I could rest for a while. I went to my classroom and sat down. Since I could still wiggle all my limbs and walk, I guessed that maybe I was okay.

I finished a couple more days of school. On the last day of school, I had my moving truck rented and was ready to move to Arkansas. My house had sold and the buyers were eager to take possession of it. All I needed to do was vacuum it out and take out the trash. I did all that and was ready to leave. My friend, took me to breakfast before I went to the school to turn in my keys. As we crossed the parking lot at the restaurant, I commented to her that my legs were hurting. She thought maybe I should see a doctor. I had no time to see a doctor and still get my belongings to Arkansas. It would just have to wait. I moved.

Two days after I got to Arkansas, Mom informed us that she was ready to move in with me. There I was, barely able to walk by then and in so much pain that I had to elevate my legs on pillows just to get to sleep at night. Now my 82-year-old mother was there, and she didn't even drive!

I had no shades or curtains up. Mom and I went shopping for them, and I came home and put them up. By the time I finished, I was not only feeling pain in my legs and left hip, but now I had sharp pain when I would take a deep breath. I didn't tell Mom about that part.

Mom and a friend were both pressuring me to see a doctor. I had just changed from regular teacher insurance to retirement insurance and wasn't even sure it had kicked in yet. Also, I wanted to be healed. I considered doctor visits such a waste of money, and I needed that money for settling in. I was afraid of being put in the hospital, and I didn't even have a doctor yet. What if they wanted to do surgery? I had to drive. Mom never learned to drive. Who would shop for our groceries? Who would get us to church? No, I would wait and see what God would do.

We were visiting churches and trying to see where we fit in. On a particular Sunday after I had suffered for three or four weeks, we were in church and the pastor asked if anyone needed prayer. I had already decided I would prayer if given the chance. When he made the invitation, Mom poked me in the side with her elbow. I said, "I'm going." I went to the front. The church ladies were gathered around me. The pastor asked my problem and had his wife to anoint me with oil. He told the ladies to put their hands on my legs. It was a strange feeling with all those hands latched on to my knees and calves of my legs, but they prayed. I didn't feel anything special.

As we left church, Mom asked if my legs felt any better. I said that I thought maybe a little. By bedtime that day they were much better. The following day I was fine—no pain, no swelling, no breathing difficulty, no leg elevation. I was healed! Praise the Lord who does all things well!

I don't know why sometimes people get healed and sometimes not. This I do know, God heals in our time and I am living proof. He leaves no scars. He is way less expensive than doctors. He doesn't just cover the symptoms with meds, but heals. It is one of the fringe benefits of living and working for the Lord.

I appreciate all that doctors do. I know they need to make a living too, and I go to them. I like to let them know when Jesus heals me. Even doctors need to know the miraculous God that we serve, but I always like to go to Dr. Jesus before Dr. Anybody Else. I do have a tendency to avoid doctors, and they sometimes get a little irritated by that.

Called to be Elsewhere

Office Assistant

Once over the injured legs and having caught up on visiting relatives that I had not had a chance to visit in years, I was ready to go back to work. A dear friend who attended my church, told me of a job opening where she worked. I filled out an application and got the job. It started as a low-salary, part-time job. It was just what I needed to give me the extra cash to contribute more to the church and take care of buying shower gifts, etc.

I worked about a year in that position and then got a position in the Contracts Administration Department of the same company. I was also classified part-time there but usually got at least 35 or more hours of work per week. To me it was full-time. I enjoyed the work most of the time. I really brushed up on my typing skills in that position. ...guess the Lord knew I would write a book someday.

I had work done on my house, contributed to our church building fund, and bought some needed appliances while I worked there. I made some lasting friendships. That was the best part.

Blessing for a Friend

After seven years at my office job, I had built up a couple of weeks of vacation and almost three weeks of sick leave. I learned by phone and e-mail of a friend who was in great need of heart surgery. I thought of all God's blessings to me and knew that He had made a way for me to help her. I was thankful that I could help. I would use my sick leave and vacation money to go to Houston and take care of her. I spoke with a couple of teacher friends, and we worked together to cover about six weeks of time with her. It was definitely a team effort, God being part of that team.

I was greatly concerned as I read scriptures and prayed for her the morning of the surgery. She had given me her clothing and valuables and lay waiting to be taken for the procedure that was to last several hours. It was extremely sobering. Our friends waited outside the room and prayed for us. Her pastor arrived about two minutes before they took her, and he prayed with us also. I was so thankful when he walked in! They whisked her away. We felt so helpless. We knew the next several hours would be slow as we waited for word from the heart surgeon and the real Keeper of her life.

We waited with and got to know some of her relatives. They would take over her care when we left. We prayed. Between conversations, I wrote a detailed report of what was happening. I wanted her to have it when she got home. The tension built to monumental proportions. At last, the doctor called us to come to the CVICU for a report on the procedure. He said she had come through it okay and was in the unit with her own personal nurse. They had replaced her aortic valve and repaired another. He stressed the importance of hand sanitation before seeing her. He told us we would be allowed to see her as soon as they got her settled.

My mom was the one who had prepared me for what I would see. She had worked 14 years at a hospital and had seen how heart surgery patients came out of surgery. She told me to expect her to be swollen—a lot. Mom was right. She was almost unrecognizable. The nurse told us to talk to her. I went near her bed and said the only thing I could think of to say, "You still have your tan." She later told me that she remembered hearing me say that. She had gone for a tan just before the surgery. I believe she thought she might not make it and didn't want to be "pale".

During my stay with her in the hospital, I prayed as I watched the medical personnel pump liter after liter of fluid from her and bag after bag of blood in. We were extremely careful about cleanliness while caring for her and sanitized again after the staff had cleaned the room. She managed to avoid infections.

It was the start of a long and heart-wrenching six months of recovery. My friends and I stayed our six weeks, taking turns caring for her. I was able to take her home for a little while at the end of my five and a half weeks. I then turned her care over to someone else and returned home.

A week later, she was back in the hospital. This time I had no money to spend to help. I prayed as the calls came in detailing the infections she had and the likelihood that she would not make it. We prayed. It was all we could do, but it was all that was needed. God took over.

Today she is at home and able to travel and enjoy her family.

> *The Lord is my shepherd...though I walk through the valley of the shadow of death, I will fear no evil: for Thou art with me; ... (Psalm 23: 1, 4)*

Midnight Serenade

For several months after I decided to return to Texas, I was serenaded nightly, at times all night long, by birds. The songs were beautiful. But they would wake me throughout the night, these songbirds. I wondered why they preferred to sing at night. It wasn't just one bird. It was bunches. I thought whatever their reasons, they sure were happy about them.

After a little time of these wake-up-calls, I decided to take some advice I had once given to Mother. I said, "When you have trouble sleeping, pray. Not only will it help you get closer to God and get prayers answered for needs you know about, it will upset the devil so much he will usually try to get you to go to sleep right away to stop it."

Have you ever noticed that when you begin to pray you will think of all kinds of "stuff" you need to get done? When you were not praying, you couldn't think of any of it.

> *To keep satan from getting the advantage over us; for we are not ignorant of his wiles and intentions. (II Cor. 2:11, Amplified Bible)*
>
> *Lest satan should get an advantage of us: for we are not ignorant of his devices. (II Cor. 2:11, KJV)*

Keep praying and the Spirit of God will help you make those intercessory prayers.

> *So too the Holy Spirit comes to our aid and bears us up in our weakness; for we do not know what prayer to offer nor how to offer it worthily as we ought, but the Spirit Himself goes to meet our supplication and pleads in our behalf with unspeakable yearnings and groanings too deep for utterance. (Romans 8:26, Amplified Bible)*

> *Likewise the Spirit also helpeth our infirmities; for we know not what we should pray for as we ought; but the Spirit itself maketh intercession for us with groanings which cannot be uttered. (Romans 8:26 (KJV)*

I realized after my praying grandma passed away that she wouldn't be around to pray for all of us anymore. I figured out that if it got done, somebody had to do it. I wasn't sure how many others were praying, so I guessed one had better be me! I won't need to pray in heaven, but I sure need to pray here. That is why I am including a little part on prayer in this writing.

Bad Housing Market

I started to feel like moving again. I told Mom that I was thinking of selling my house and taking an apartment. I even checked on an apartment with two bedrooms and a one-car garage, but they would not allow me to have two dogs. I already had two dogs and loved both and didn't want to lose either of them. Mom was always telling me that I had better not sell my house. She would always say, "You'll be sorry!" So I settled in, I thought, to stay. The more I planned to stay the more unsettled I felt. After a while I told Mom, "I have given this my best shot. It hasn't worked. I'm going to sell this house and move back to Texas."

Then everybody was saying, "The housing market is down. You may not be able to sell. Lots of houses have been sitting on the market for years without selling." I listened, and I prayed and gave it to the Lord. I even wrote the prayer on a piece of paper in my prayer book. If it didn't sell that was fine, but I felt I should put it on the market, and I did.

I had a six-month contract with the realtor. Even she gave me the talk about the market when she took my house. She said there were lots of new houses on the market that were in the price range that my house was and many times people would choose a new house over an older one. My house was seven years old. I listened.

I watched some properties in a couple of different parts of Texas. I liked the looks of both of them online. Well, we would cross that bridge if or when we needed to.

My house was showing, but no offers. We lowered the price a little. The realtor had set it a bit higher than even I thought we should. She expected the prospective buyers to want us to come off the asking price a little. Time rocked on and we got a ridiculously low offer. I told her, "No way! I can't give it away. I have to have a place to live when I'm done with this."

A few days before the contract expired, the realtor said she hoped I would allow her to keep it. We had listed it in September. She said that maybe it would show better in the spring. I made no comment, but planned to give it to someone else for a shorter amount of time. Then if it didn't sell, I would have my answer from the Lord.

Two days before my contract was out, my realtor called me to say she was sending a person to look at my house. She said it would be late when they came. I did the usual cleaning touch-ups, grabbed the dogs and left the house. We returned after dark, and I was just settling in for the night when the phone rang. I answered and my realtor said, "The lady who looked at your house fell in love with it!" She said that the lady had been preapproved for the selling price. A couple of days later she called to tell me that I would need to be out by the end of March which only gave me about three and a half weeks. I said okay. I thought I might have to move into storage, but my house was sold!

My brother and I made a quick trip to Texas to see some of the houses I had been watching online that were in my price range. They were a bit smaller, but it was okay if I had to downsize. They looked great online but horrible in the real world! My feathers fell, so to speak. My niece drove out to meet us for lunch where we were looking. She accompanied us to see a couple of houses. We all agreed that they were bad.

I had a plan B, and it was beginning to look like I might need it. If I couldn't find a suitable house I would return to the town I had been living in and rent an apartment. I would leave one of my little dogs with a friend and take him for his shots when he needed them. I could buy his dog food, visit him, etc.

My niece said if I would consider a place near her, she could call a friend who would refer us to a realtor that would see what she could do for us. If, if, if... I gave her my own list of if's and expected nothing because the list was rather long: if they could be seen today, if they were in my price range, if they had very small yards, if they had fenced back yards, if they were near good churches, if they were not in the middle of the city, if they were near her family...

She made her calls and by the time we arrived on her side of town there were seven houses lined up for us to see. We looked at all but one. The one we did not see could only be shown on Sunday. It didn't matter. We already had our minds made up. We all liked the first one we saw. I thought it would not be something I could afford, but because of a foreclosure it was.

We had not planned to spend the night, but when we were pretty sure things would work out, we borrowed grooming articles and spent the night at my niece's home. The next day we did all the necessary paperwork to get the process started.

> *...be strong, and very courageous, that you may do according to all the law...*

...Turn not from it to the right hand or to the left, that you may prosper wherever you go.

This book of the law shall not depart out of your mouth, but you shall meditate on it day and night, that you may observe and do according to all that is written in it; for then you shall make your way prosperous, and then you shall deal wisely and have good success.

...be strong, vigorous, and very courageous; be not afraid, neither be dismayed; for the Lord your God is with you wherever you go.

...for the Lord your God, He is God in Heaven above, and on earth beneath.

(Joshua 1:7-9, 2:11)

Praises to my Jesus!

Beginning to Understand

Songs

I have no doubt that some of the best songs are born during a storm in someone's life. I do not know the background of the song I will tell about in this experience in my life, but it would not surprise me to find that the above is true for it.

God gave me an opportunity to move from Dallas, TX, to The Valley to get experience working with bilingual students. I really loved the Spanish language and teaching Hispanic students. I learned so much from them; I saw immense talent and potential that I wanted to help develop. With this move, I left a small but strong church and went to a church that was struggling to build a new building and win new souls to the Lord. They were also struggling to keep the ones they had. At first, one sweet elderly lady and I were the only ones who came to prayer meetings on Saturday evenings. We had some great prayer meetings, and later others started joining us in prayer. Still, I sometimes missed the presence of God that I often felt in the Dallas church.

On a certain occasion, I had the chance to visit my old church. I was excited about that. I hoped for an outpouring of God's Spirit in the services, especially for my own refreshing. The service was good, but it was nothing like I had seen in the past. I returned to The Valley disappointed.

I got back into my routines at work and at church. I kept on working for my Lord, but I felt rather unproductive.

One day or night at church, I can't remember which; I was worshipping with a song of praise that was being sung. It wasn't that I had never heard this song before. In fact, it was an old song. The way it was sung was nothing out of the ordinary. But the truth of the words suddenly hit me with such an impact that the Spirit of the Lord was all over me! I was getting that refreshing I so much desired, right there where I was living! When I finally was able to open my eyes, I was standing out in the isle to the left and several rows up from where I had been sitting. I was facing the wall, weeping, rejoicing, and praising God! The rest of the people were also being mightily blessed. There were several new converts after that service. God knows what to send and when to send it, and He is always on time.

That song, which was not special to me before, is now one of my all-time favorites. Sometimes I sing the parts I know over and over to myself and to God at home. I hope He enjoys it as much as I do.

* * * * * * * *

I am thankful for all the modern ways of projecting songs on screens and letting congregations sing along, but I wish we still had hymnals to take home or buy and keep at home. There is something to be said for being able to repeatedly go to a certain song that ministers to us and brings glory to God and have it at our fingertips. Singing and worship can be an at-home thing as well as an at-church thing if we have the words and the music with us. We eventually commit the words to memory and they are ours for the rest of our lives. Some of that one is mine.

Prayer

Some of my prayer teachers were Grandma, Pastor and Sister Green, Sister Torres, and Pastor and Sister Gaddy. Each of these taught me something different about praying. I will share some of it with you.

I learned from Grandma not to make excuses for not praying. Grandma usually whispered her prayers those times that I heard her pray. I was at Mom and Dad's once for a few weeks. Grandma just happened to be visiting at the same time. The living room was warm but the bedrooms were ice-cold. I slept in the bedroom with Grandma. We would get ready for bed and rush to our cold bedroom and under the covers as fast as we could! After we were in bed, I would hear Grandma whispering her prayers. It was a comforting sound.

Pastor and Sister Green taught me that prayer is made after requests are presented, and God meets those needs. The church usually set aside an hour one night a week for "prayer meeting". We would have everyone who came to present any special needs they had or knew about. Sometimes it took 15 or 20 minutes to hear the requests. We would start praying and pray for the rest of the time. Pastor Green would sometimes take some extra time at the end to bring needs with a broader scope, and we would all pray for those. When I first started attending, I did well to pray five or ten minutes; but as I listened to my pastor and his wife pray aloud, I realized that they were praying for each person's request. How did they remember all that? They were so specific. Sister So-and-so needed healing of diabetes, Brother Thus-and-So needed a job, etc. I kind of worked out a system of praying at prayer meetings that worked for me.

- Listen, and take mental notes during request time.
- Notice where each person is located so you can visualize them in prayer and know when you have covered every request.
- Pray thanks to God for prayers He has already answered.
- Don't hurry.
- Pray for one request at a time and be specific without lumping them together (lumping ex: Bless all my brothers and sisters.)
- Pray for your own needs and requests.
- Listen to the preacher pray. If you run out of prayers before others, you can lend your prayer support to his prayers. He will even know of some needs not named in the request time but just as important.
- Be quiet and listen for God's prayer request. Pray about those.
- Thank God for the freedom and privilege of prayer.
- Watch and listen for answers to your prayers, and be thankful.

July 21, 1988, Sister Green taught our ladies group a lesson called "When You Pray for the Saints". She took her study from Ephesians 4. I still refer to these scriptures to determine what God wants us to pray for each other. These scriptures give us a good picture of what God wants his children to be. We can pray for that.

My precious Sister Torres taught me patience and persistence in prayer, and that others notice your approach to prayer, even when it doesn't seem like it. When I first started going to church with her, she was the only one who came to prayer meeting. She had a key to the church and was always there for Saturday night prayer. When I got there, that made two. We had some outstanding prayer services. Others started to join us after a while. Before long our prayer room was pretty full.

Pastor and Sister Gaddy helped deepen my belief that God hears your conversational tone just as He does your pleading and begging tone. Pastor Gaddy said that as his child's dad, if she came to him whining her requests to him, he would likely have her calm down and just tell him her need. She wouldn't be any more likely to get her need met by begging. He is her dad. He wants to give her what she needs. Of course there are times of urgency, and it **will show**. But making requests can be done in a calm way.

I enjoyed listening to Pastor Gaddy pray before he preached. The prayers were very specific and practical. He prayed for himself and his delivery of the message God had given him. He prayed for the hearers to understand and act on his words. I saw God's answers time after time. We kept the water ready in the baptismal tank and frequently baptized during the Sunday morning service.

Sister Gaddy taught me to ask for and expect the impossible. When I arrived at the church where the Gaddys pastored, services were held in a store front and about 35 attended on a good Sunday. God was blessing, and soon we were having two services to get everybody in. We rented part of an antique mall to have more space. The owners made it very clear from the beginning that it was not for sale. During a special service, the evangelist asked each of us to stand and name something seemingly impossible that we wanted God to do. Sister Gaddy said she wanted us to be able to buy the building we were renting.

Several months passed, and we outgrew the space we rented. We were again having two services to get everybody in. We looked into buying another large building that was in need of a lot of remodel work. The deal fell through, and the sale went to someone else. Finally, the owners of our rental, after repeatedly saying that the property was not for sale, called Pastor Gaddy and said they had changed their minds. They were ready to sell if we still wanted to buy. We did! Church services are now being held in the newly remodeled building. Praise the Lord!

Some Practical Prayer Starters:

- Thankfulness
- Bible reading and praying the Word

(Once I prayed an entire chapter for my brother, and God answered my prayer!)

- Needs
- Blessings
- Requests
- Songs
- News
- Sermons
- Individual salvation needs
- Group needs (church, military, care groups and ministries, youth, leaders, countries, missions, etc.)

Prayer Approaches:

Say it, shout it, write it, whisper it, cry it, groan it, plead it, utter it in the Holy Spirit, list it…

…but **PRAY!**

It is not about how long or short the prayer is, **but it is about how sincere and focused it is**. God is listening and watching. Prayer shows Him that we believe He **can** and **will** answer. Everybody needs something that they can't have without God's help. You're His child. He will help you with that.

Can't you almost see Him coming to your prayer time and saying, "Here, let me help you with that!" ☺

He can handle it!

Memorable Sermons

"Good Ole Repentance"—Pastor Warren Green

This message was a reminder of the blessing of being able to bring a sin-sick soul to Jesus, repent of whatever made it sick, and be completely forgiven and made clean. It is never to be taken for granted; but oh, what an assurance and blessing to know there is **hope** because of the precious blood of the Master! We do not have to die lost. Our forgiveness was paid for by Jesus who suffered and died for **our** sins.

"Some on Boards, and Some on Broken Pieces of the Ship"—Pastor Tim Gaddy

The ship **will** make it to its destination. No matter what you have to do, stay with the ship. The message was taken from Acts 27:31, 44. The man of God, Paul, had warned the people on the ship with him to stay with the ship and there would not be any loss of life. Brother Gaddy compared it to the ship of today that is headed to heaven. It **will** make it. Even if you have to grab a board or some other piece of the ship, don't ever let go. Don't let anything distract or deter you. **You will make it if you stay with the ship!**

"Take Leave of Your Senses"—Pastor Jeff Arnold

Nobody wants to be told that they have taken leave of their senses. We depend on them to learn about everything around us. However, when it comes to the things of God, they are not understood by the senses. They are spiritually discerned, so we have to take leave of our senses and trust God. Proverbs 3:5-6. I did not attend the service where this message was preached. A friend brought the tape to me from a service she attended. I have listened to it numerous times. Those of us from the "educated" group like the logical and understandable. I have shared this tape with some of my Ph.D. educated friends with a feeling of assurance that they would be able to identify with the message.

Pastors, you never know where your messages will end up!

Just keep preaching!

Acts 13: 40-41 Amplified Bible

40: *Take care, therefore, lest there come upon you what is spoken in the prophets.*
41: *Look, you scoffers and scorners, and marvel, and perish, and vanish away; for I am doing a deed in your days, a deed which you will never have confidence in or believe, [even] if someone— clearly describing it in detail—declares it to you.*

Acts13:40-41 Holy Bible KJV

40: *Beware therefore, lest that come upon you, which is spoken of in the prophets;*
41: *Behold ye despisers, and wonder, and perish: for I work a work in your days, a work which ye shall in no wise believe, though a man declare it unto you.*

Habakkuk 1:5

Behold ye among the heathen, and wonder marvelously; for I will work a work in your days, which ye will not believe, though it be told you.